Struggle and Suffrage
in
Glasgow

Struggle and Suffrage in Glasgow

Women's Lives and the Fight for Equality

By Judith Vallely

PEN & SWORD
HISTORY

AN IMPRINT OF PEN & SWORD BOOKS LTD
YORKSHIRE - PHILADELPHIA

First published in Great Britain in 2019 by
Pen & Sword History
An imprint of
Pen & Sword Books Ltd
Yorkshire – Philadelphia

ISBN 978 1 52671 8 297

Printed and bound in England
by 4edge Ltd, Essex, SS5 4AD
Typeset in 11.5/14 point Times New Roman
by Aura Technology and Software Services, India

Pen & Sword Books Limited incorporates the imprints of Atlas,
Archaeology, Aviation, Discovery, Family History, Fiction, History,
Maritime, Military, Military Classics, Politics, Select, Transport, True
Crime, Air World, Frontline Publishing, Leo Cooper, Remember When,
Seaforth Publishing, The Praetorian Press, Wharncliffe Local History,
Wharncliffe Transport, Wharncliffe True Crime and White Owl.

For a complete list of Pen & Sword titles please contact
PEN & SWORD BOOKS LIMITED
47 Church Street, Barnsley, South Yorkshire, S70 2AS, England
E-mail: enquiries@pen-and-sword.co.uk
Website: www.pen-and-sword.co.uk

Or
PEN AND SWORD BOOKS
1950 Lawrence Rd, Havertown, PA 19083, USA
E-mail: Uspen-and-sword@casematepublishers.com
Website: www.penandswordbooks.com

Contents

For Mum

Introduction: 'The Door is Open'

A century ago, a young oak tree was planted in a ceremony at Kelvingrove Park in Glasgow. The event was witnessed by a gathering of women, dressed in the bright colours of the Suffragettes – purple for loyalty and dignity, white for purity and green for hope. It marked the passing of the Representation of the People Act on the 6 February 1918, which allowed some women the right to vote. The success came only after a long campaign which became infamous for violent protests and actions, hunger strikes and force-feeding and the death of a woman in front of the king's horse.

The ceremony took place in the closing months of the First World War. The speakers were clear about the significance of the act – but also the fact that the battle for equality was far from over. The legislation only applied to women over the age of 30 who met certain criteria, while the same act gave all men over the age of 21 the right to vote, abolishing previous property and other restrictions. Now some women could have a say in elections if they were aged over 30 and a householder – or married to one – or a university graduate aged over 21. It added up to 8.5 million women across the UK, but still represented only 40 per cent of the female population.[1] Yet it was an important step forward.

Several women's suffrage organisations took part in the tree planting ceremony, showing just how varied and widespread the activities were in the city. They included the Glasgow Society for Women's Suffrage, the Scottish Universities Women's Suffrage Union, the Women's Freedom League, the Conservative and Unionist Women's Franchise Association and the United Suffragists. The oak was planted by Louisa Lumsden, a leading suffragist and pioneer of women's education who later became a Dame. She summed it up as she declared: 'The vote is the door to everything, and the door is open. At the same time it is not wholly open, for the younger women are still excluded, but I think you can't get Governments to go at a tremendous pace.' She added, 'To the younger women I would say: "Have patience and prepare yourselves, for you cannot be too good for the possible opportunities that may come in the future.'"[2]

For women who did qualify to vote, the first experience of the ballot box came in the same year that oak tree was planted. It happened on 14 December 1918, in the general election which was called after the ending of the First World War. The polling day was on a Saturday. World news making the headlines that day included US President Woodrow Wilson landing in Brest, France for a visit to the country. Closer to home, there was a report of a court case involving an alleged attempt to bribe Crown officials in order to purchase two of the smallest of the Channel Islands. Another newspaper story noted that shopkeepers in London who during the war had 'seemed to shed all the politeness which was once regarded as an essential part of the art of salesmanship' were now returning to more courteous ways. The Church of Scotland urged better allowances for sailors, soldiers and their families and in Glasgow improvements being made to the river Clyde to rid the river of sewage and rubbish were applauded. In the listings for situations vacant, job adverts included for bakers, boat-builders, message boys, grocers, hairdressers, shorthand typists and waitresses. Numerous domestic servant roles were also advertised, from cooks and maids to housekeepers and nurses, showing a high demand for household workers at the time.[3]

Against this background, and the turbulent backdrop of the aftermath of war, women headed to the ballot box for the first time across Britain. They included centenarian Mrs 'Granny' Lambert, of Edmonton, London, who was reported to be 105 years old.[4] On the opposite end of the age scale, in the same borough a girl aged 9½ years old was said to be discovered to be on the voting register late in the evening. When her parents were told she could vote, she was 'hurried out of bed and rushed off to the polling booth.'[5]

Despite fears of apathy among the newly enfranchised women – with commentators noting poor attendances at candidate meetings in the run-up to polling day – the large number of female voters was seen as an outstanding feature of the election, which was on a day with generally fine weather. 'Everywhere they showed a determination to record their votes, one way or another', noted one newspaper report. 'This feature was especially noticeable in the towns. Women of all social positions took their part in the election. The working man's wife, often carrying the youngest child, was much in evidence at some of the Glasgow polling booths...'[6] In Dumbarton, women also helped as clerks, with voting papers dropped into boxes made out of shell cases.[7]

Steady streams of women, attending in twos and threes and often dressed in their 'Sunday best' clothes, went to the polls in Glasgow. The new voting rights meant that the electorate grew from 194,171 to 524,006 in the city, with women accounting for 194,332 of that figure.[8] There was little election literature aimed at women, according to reports, with one exception being a cartoon of a naked baby with outstretched arms and the message 'Mothers, vote for Labour', in Maryhill. However, the only woman candidate in Scotland, Eunice Murray, who stood as an independent in Glasgow's Bridgeton Division, chose an unusual way to catch the attention of voters with the use of a rhyme, 'Better housing, better health/Better work, better wealth/Better laws, better land/Better let women take a hand/So vote for Murray!'[9]

For the women who were now able to cast their votes, descriptions of the atmosphere of the city polling booths show them relishing the occasion: 'They were among the earliest arrivals at the poll, and many of them, doubtless appreciating the historical significance of the moment, brought their offspring with them, children in arms even, and with these precious burdens they made their mark...'[10]

An account of an anonymous Glasgow woman's experience of voting was published in the *Daily Record* under the title 'Her First Vote, By Puzzled Wife'.[11] She described it as 'difficult as filling in a ration book', not in terms of the process of voting, but in deciding which candidate she should back. 'My father, a strong Radical, had brought me up on Liberal principles; the newspapers advised me to vote Coalition; while personally I had a rather warm side to the Labour party,' she wrote. 'To add to the confusion, my husband was a "die-hard" Conservative, who wished to run an independent candidate...The whole thing was as complicated as a divorce case.' She says that she was so anxious to vote conscientiously, she believes she even lost weight during the last week of the election and inside the polling booth describes: 'a delicious sense of importance. My first vote.'

It wasn't until the Equal Franchise Act of 1928 that women finally had full equality with men on the issue of voting, when suffrage was extended to all women over the age of 21. It wasn't until 1970 that the voting age was lowered to 18 for both sexes in the UK. Key to winning suffrage had been the success of women who took on work during the First World War, proving that they were as capable as men.

When the bill allowing the enfranchisement of women was passed in the House of Lords in 1918, the *Britannia* newspaper of the Women's Party, edited by Christabel Pankhurst, one of the driving forces of the Suffragette movement, noted the significance of the event in a front page editorial. The new legislation had been passed just over fifty years after the issue of women's suffrage had first been seriously raised in Parliament by an MP:

'Half a century has elapsed since John Stuart Mill asked Parliament to give the vote to women and since the House of Commons soon after carried a Second reading of a Woman Suffrage Bill. The pioneer women who began the movement for women's emancipation have nearly all passed away – noble hearts who were inspired and rewarded, not by victory for themselves, but by the certain faith that the women who came after them would see victory.

'Later when the Votes for Women cause seemed to the ordinary world dead and forgotten, came the militant movement, in which women faced opprobrium, sacrificed their personal liberty, and even gave their life to win the vote.

'Then followed the war, whereupon militancy was laid aside. The militants took to national war service and claimed for women the right of war service in new forms, in addition to the time-honoured and valuable nursing and the like.

'The splendid national service rendered by British women as a whole – by those outside as well as those inside the various Suffrage organisations – has finally proved not only that every argument against women's enfranchisement is null and void, but also that women's handwork and brainwork and women's devotion and public spirit are needed for the salvation and redemption of the country.'[12]

The suffragette movement had of course, been instrumental in women winning the right to vote. And it is the most high-profile names and events that have lingered long in history; from the leadership of the Pankhurst sisters – Emmeline and her daughters Christabel and Sylvia – to the women who went on hunger strike and then suffered the brutality of force feeding, to the shocking death of Emily Davison when she was knocked down by the king's horse at Epsom Derby. However, women across the country were involved in these kind of activities – including in Glasgow, where militancy resulted in attacks on the city's landmarks and buildings, a meeting which ended in a riot and even an attempt to cut off the city's water supply.

It would also be wrong to characterise the fight for suffrage just as a violent campaign – or indeed one that had taken place only in the immediate years running up to the First World War. Although that was when the movement reached a peak, women had been on a quest for equality and improvements in society for decades beforehand, from challenging employment conditions to battling for the right to access university education and entering medical and healthcare professions for the first time. These changes were happening across Britain and included many pioneering women of Glasgow who both fought for the vote and for wider changes in society. Their achievements and lives will be explored in chapters to come.

The group of women gathered round to witness the planting of a young oak tree a century ago in Kelvingrove Park, could not have foreseen just how far their actions would reverberate in the years to come and change their world – and ours – forever. After all, who can predict how actions taken now will ripple through the centuries? But it is clear they were fully aware of the significance of the events:

> Miss Frances Melville, BD, Glasgow, who presided, said they had met to commemorate what was perhaps the most important change ever made in the British Constitution; also to see a memorial set in the great heart of a great city. The enfranchisement of women would bring a new life into the body politic, and therefore it was most appropriate to plant in commemoration a living and a growing thing.[13]

Today the city of Glasgow is, of course, much changed from that of the early twentieth century. Once it thrummed with industry and shipbuilding, now it bustles with modern architecture and tourists. But walking through the streets it is still possible to see the remnants of the past and glimpses into the city of a century ago. On Queen Margaret Drive, there is a building which is now most well-known for being home to the BBC for decades, but was once the foundation of first university education for women in Glasgow. The ornate and striking entrance to the Mitchell Library today used to be the façade of St Andrew's Halls, a former concert venue which was the scene of a stormy suffragette meeting which ended in a riot. And if you walk along Kelvin Way towards Glasgow University, just a few metres to the left of the pavement, the suffragette tree still stands, albeit battered and damaged by storms. From small beginnings, it is now a tall oak tree which has endured and grown for decades – much like the campaign for women's suffrage and equality to which it was planted in tribute.

CHAPTER ONE

Education:
'Keep Knocking at the Gates'

More than half of students in higher education in Scotland are now women – accounting for 57 per cent of the overall total.[1] So it's perhaps difficult to imagine that just over a century ago, the doors of such institutions were firmly closed to women. Scotland underwent a boom in educational growth in the nineteenth century, with the introduction of compulsory elementary lessons for all children aged between 5 and 13 years old in 1872. Yet opportunities for female pupils were still very limited, with most of the focus in their education being on preparing for work in industry, service or the home.[2] The development of secondary schools for girls and advent of serious academic schooling for them, however, encouraged more middle-class families to consider that their daughters might be as academically able as their sons, and not just destined for a life of domesticity.

The Glasgow Ladies' Higher Education Association was one of the organisations helping to push forward the idea that indeed, women would benefit from participating in education for longer. In an address to the University of Glasgow in 1914, one of the founders, David Murray, a lawyer, noted how Scotland had never been without women of culture – in the form of poetesses, songwriters, dramatists and novelists. But he also pointed out that culture and learning could, for a long time, only be gained through private study – either self-taught or taught by a male relative who had the advantage of an extensive education. 'A woman's education ended with school: the gates of the universities were closed to her,' Murray said. In the address he went on to cite the 'oft-repeated advice' of Professor Edward Caird, a member of the Queen Margaret College council and a supporter of the women's education movement to 'keep knocking at the gates until they are opened'.[3] It is a fitting symbol for the persistent efforts that women had to make, in order to gain access through those university gates.

There had been some notable exceptions to the idea that higher education classes were not a suitable place for women. In the late eighteenth century, Dr Thomas Garnett, the first Professor of Natural Philosophy at Anderson's Institution – an antecedent of the University of Strathclyde – had thrown open his classes to women. By 1797, nearly 1,000 students, around half of whom were women, had attended lectures on topics such as chemistry and philosophy. By the 1830s and 1840s, female students could take up a number of classes in subjects such as French and mathematics, but crucially it was only done on a very informal basis and they could not proceed to graduation.[4]

With impetus growing around learning and advances of the day in the sphere of the home, which meant women of higher social classes had more free time, came a growing desire to participate in education. Even the humble sewing machine was instrumental in changing women's lives, according to Jessie Campbell, who was born in 1827 and was one of the pioneers of education for women in Glasgow.

She noted that:

> The sewing machine has been one of the great emancipators of women from the dreary round of household needlework. This was a great occupation for indigent gentlewomen, but the daughters of families had a large share of it, and to make a shirt was considered a necessary accomplishment.[5]

However, Campbell wryly notes that the freeing up of time brought with it a notion of having 'more than they knew what to do with', resulting in what she described as a 'dreary' existence.

So the languid invalidish lady became the fashion, and fainting upon all occasions, whether trying to the nervous system, or not, was thought becoming to a gentlewoman! Extreme chaperonage, and the dependence upon their menkind to which women were subjected, made life at that period very dreary. Education beyond a limited amount was discouraged, and to write books was thought most unbecoming to the position of women of rank.[6]

The idea of admitting women to the University of Glasgow was first mooted in 1868, during a dinner party held at the house of a professor. After dinner the women in the drawing room discussed the idea of having a course of lectures. Campbell describes how she was the one who was volunteered into asking one of the professors to give a course of lectures on English literature to women. The response, she notes, was initially less than promising, and illustrates well the attitude of the time that university education was not befitting for women:

I well remember how he shook back his fine head, and with astonished looks said: 'I lecture to ladies. No-one would come and listen to me; the thing is preposterous.' However, by great persuasion, we got him to consider the matter, and the result was a large enthusiastic audience and a most brilliant course of lectures. They were delivered in the Corporation Galleries, and were open to gentlemen as well as to ladies. This was really the introduction to the Higher and University education of women; it was the first time lectures were given by the special request of women, and earnestness was shewn [sic] by having them continued.[7]

The impetus for this 'unofficial' university education, which began later in the same year of the dinner party, was no doubt spurred on by informal lectures for women which had been delivered in Edinburgh the previous year. In addition, there were other places in the world where such an advance had been made decades before; Oberlin College in Ohio, USA, for example, opened its doors to women in 1833[8], a full half a century before Scotland took such radical steps.

For around a decade, these informal lectures were regularly held, triggering a growing interest in the higher education of women. The cause took a step forward when the Glasgow Association for the Higher Education of Women was formed in 1877. The founders included some prominent women in the west of Scotland and the president was Princess Louise, the daughter of Queen Victoria. It also had the backing of influential men, including the university principal John Caird.[9] It had the stated mission of both making courses available and the wider promotion of the higher education of women. The very first session of the association was held in November 1877, with topics including French literature, logic and natural history:

> Lectures have been delivered to ladies by several of our University Professors for a number of years, and the association now formed, consisting largely of ladies who have been in the habit of attending those lectures, desire to carry on the work thus begun in a more systematic form and to a greater extent.[10]

At last, it seemed, attitudes to women's education as something which was not required and would even impact on their marriage prospects and 'womanly nature' appeared to be slowly changing. An account of the annual meeting of the association two years later noted: 'The notion that education, except of the most flimsy sort, has a hardening and roughening effect on women is now pretty well exploded.'[11]

It went on:

> That it lessens their chances in the marriage market is an idea now confined to a few ignorant mothers, who according to a late Schools' Inquiry Report, still perplex teachers with injunctions such as – 'Keep Julia to her music, but never mind the arithmetic; her husband will do her sums for her...' It may be quite true that the 'wife and mother' sphere is the true and natural one for women and it is a sphere which few of them show any disinclination for when the opportunity presents itself; but setting aside the fact that this opportunity does not always

present itself, it is now seen that a higher education cannot make them less, but more fit for it.

Lectures offered at that time ranged from the philosophy of religion and German literature to music theory and domestic economy. While distance learning may seem a modern invention, the association offered 'instruction by correspondence' so that women living in the countryside could participate in classes.

In 1882, the annual meeting of the association outlined the progress which had been made. There were 283 students enrolled in correspondence classes, with pupils in 'many parts of the Continent and in India'.[12] Bursaries were offered to students by the association, and a Governess Loan Fund was set up to provide grants to women who were teachers, or preparing to be teachers, to pay for classes and examination fees.

Professor John Caird, principal of Glasgow University, however, noted that public support for the association had been but 'languid and stinted'. He put forward arguments to counteract the prejudices surrounding the higher education of women which still seemed to persist.

He said:

> It has, I know, sometimes been alleged that the strain of university studies and examinations under which male students break down would be too severe for the great majority of girls. But the answer is obvious. A system of education which breaks down the health of either boys or girls, would indeed be self-condemned, but the objection here is one which applies not to the use but to the abuse of the studies in question. Work or employment of any kind may run to excess. Social engagements, balls, evening parties may be good enough in moderation, but they may be and sometimes are indulged to such an excess as to do more damage to a girl's health than any amount of hard study which the average women is likely to engage in.[13]

Professor Caird went on to dismiss the 'old and ungallant stock assertions as to the intellectual inferiority of women'. But even the most progressive attitudes of the day only went so far – as he raised doubts about the suitability of women entering a number of 'male' professions:

> There will always remain a large number of employments and avocations of which the more robust sex will retain a monopoly. I for one never wish to see, nor I believe you wish to see, female attorneys or engineers, or magistrates or members of Parliament. (Applause)… But, on the other hand, as long as the influence of women is what it is and must be, it is the interest of society to make her something more than the domestic drudge or the domestic ornament, the minister to man's comforts or the plaything of his hours of idleness.[14]

The association offered courses of study which could be taken over six years and certificates which aimed to meet university standards. In 1883, it was established as Queen Margaret College – after Saint Margaret of Scotland, the eleventh century and first ever Queen of Scots. It was the first women's college in Scotland, but still a few decades behind England, where the similar institutions had first been set up in the 1840s.[15]

However, the college still did not have a home. That was to change when Isabella Elder, a wealthy philanthropist who donated much time and money to campaigning for women's education, gifted the house and grounds of North Park House.

A newspaper report on 10 January 1884 noted that: 'Mrs John Elder has purchased Northpark House, Hillhead, and has intimated her intention of handing it over…to be used as a college in connection with the Glasgow Association for the Higher Education of Women.' The report also noted that at that stage around £5,000 had been raised out of £20,000 endowment fund, which Elder had stipulated must be set up to ensure the college was financially independent in the longer term.[16]

Isabella Elder, born in 1928, was the daughter of a Glasgow lawyer and married John Elder in 1857 at the age of 29. Her husband was a shipbuilder whose work was known throughout the world, with his firm building ships for the Pacific Steam Navigation

Company and the British and African Steamship Company. He died at the age of just 45, leaving Isabella to run alone, for a short time, what was one of the biggest shipyards in the world, with a workforce of nearly 5000.[17] She subsequently devoted herself to philanthropic projects, which included the setting up of a chair of naval architecture at Glasgow University, establishing a School of Domestic Economy in Govan and creating Elder Park, where a statue stands in her memory; one of only a handful of statues of women in Scotland.

Elder gifted the 37-acre Elder Park to the community of Govan in 1885. It still exists as one of Glasgow's many 'green spaces' today. It stands opposite the site of Govan's major shipbuilders, and it's easy to imagine workers throughout the years escaping at the end of the day for a relaxing wander round the paths of the park. The opening ceremony was described in colourful scenes in contemporary reports of the day:

> Strangers eager to get the best possible view of the procession were pouring in by the various conveyances – by train, ferry steamer, car, and on foot: and those who were to take part in the demonstration were hurrying to the respective muster grounds. At times it was with difficulty that pedestrians were able to get along, while vehicular traffic was almost entirely suspended. At one, by the proclamation of the Magistrates, carriages were prohibited from using the principal thoroughfares. As the day advanced the crowd increased, and perched on all the available places were spectators watching the proceedings, while thousands lined the streets along the route of the procession. Never in its history did the burgh present such a gay appearance. Govan Road, from Copeland Road to the entrance to the Park, was completely and very attractively decorated. At Copeland Road there was a red banner the whole width of the thoroughfare on which was inscribed – '3000 children heartily welcome Mrs Elder'.[18]

The ceremony was also attended by Lord Rosebery, Archibald Primrose, who went on to have a short-lived spell in office as prime minister from 1894 to 1895. He praised her contribution to society, and made the welcome observation that as a woman she was 'no less a great citizen'.

> This is not Mrs Elder's first act of munificence in this neighbourhood. (Hear, hear). She has given the Chair of Naval Architecture and Marine Engineering, which is to do much for the safety of those that go down to the sea in ships. (Hear, hear). She has given the Queen Margaret College, which is to do for the education of women what was so sorely wanted in Scotland. (Cheers). And now she has crowned her good works with the saving of this beautiful tract of ground from the hand of the builder, and handing it over for ever for the recreation of the great working classes of this burgh. (Cheers.)…Honour to this great citizen, not the less a great citizen because she is a woman, and more so because it is to a woman's heart that she owes the impulse and instinct to do these acts of munificent goodness. (Cheers.)…She is determined that the name of Elder should be not less famous for generosity than for genius, and I think you will agree with me she had accomplished her object. (Cheers.)[19]

Thanks to the generosity of Isabella Elder, Queen Margaret College came into being at North Park House in 1884. Initially there were 240 students, primarily studying the Arts, but demand was soon increasing for science courses. Medical teaching got underway in 1890, but with the basement kitchen of the college having to be used for dissection. The unsatisfactory arrangement meant efforts were soon underway to raise funds for a medical school.[20]

At this point, it was clear that much progress had been made from the days when the gates of the universities were firmly shut to women. But there were still stark differences to how the female students were treated, they could not formally graduate from university. As Jessie Campbell pointed out, there was great dissatisfaction among the female students who were attending the college that they were far from being on an equal footing to their male counterparts:

They offered us certificates, and many thought we should be satisfied with them; but it seemed hard to exact the same work and give an inferior reward, and we could not accept a lower standard. It is one of men's highest ambitions to have letters added to their names as evidence of intellectual rank, and it is natural that women who attain the same position should desire the same honours, especially when entering professional work.[21]

The Glasgow Association for the Higher Education of Women worked with others interested in advancing women's education, including in Edinburgh, to petition for an Act of Parliament to allow Scottish universities to grant degrees to women. The Medical Act of 1876 prohibited the exclusion of women from universities and medical schools but the way was finally paved with the Universities (Scotland) Act 1889, which introduced regulations for the instruction of women.

The first appearance of women scholars in lectures was, according to the first female students, greeted with a mixture of both amusement and scepticism over their abilities. Annie McMillan, one of the first to attend the university, said that the lecturers were 'amused as much by our ways as we by theirs', and on both sides the 'amusement verged sometimes on annoyance'. She recounted a lecture given by one young gentleman, who had since become a professor in a neighbouring university, who apologised to his class for the feebleness of one of his lectures by 'remarking naively that it had been "prepared for the weaker intellects of Queen Margaret College"'.

She also said:

Another lecturer afforded us unmitigated amusement by requesting that the large mirror at the end of the lecture halls should be draped, because he thought his reflection upon its surface might have a disconcerting effect upon us! Excellent youth! Had he only known it, some of his reflections upon the margin of our exercises disconcerted us ten times more. On a particularly windy March day, the entire College was thrown into intense excitement by the sudden demand made by a professor for a comb, by which to reduce his somewhat poetic locks to order. By such agreeable episodes was our way cheered in the middle ages.[22]

Annie McMillan also recounts the formation of the Debating Society on 21 December 1885. The first regular meeting to debate the 'not very exciting motion' that 'novel reading is beneficial', was held on 11 January 1886. However, a far more contentious event for the society came very soon afterwards at the time when Queen Margaret College was in the process of becoming affiliated to the University of Glasgow. It seems officials feared that an outspoken debate by women could jeopardise the acceptance among the wider public of allowing them access to higher education. Such fears provoke the question of what the debate would be about, a highly controversial call for women's rights, perhaps? In fact the subject matter was a discussion of the literary position of poet and novelist Rudyard Kipling, famous for works such as *The Jungle Book* and *The Man Who Would Be King*. Even so, the women, in the end, were not allowed to fully take part, as McMillan recounts:

> At the eleventh hour the powers that [be] stepped in and ordained that if the debate went on at all it must do so in a mutilated fashion, namely, that we of the College might write our papers, but that we could not be permitted to read them. We were advised that as affiliation of College to University was in the air, it was a critical moment in our history, and that if we persisted in supporting our own opinions in our own persons, we must prejudice the public against the cause of higher education.
>
> We bowed to these sentiments, and had the doubtful pleasure of hearing our papers read by members of the Dialectic Society – albeit they were excellent readers. Notwithstanding these little drawbacks, our evening at the Union was an entertaining one, and the courtesy of our numerous hosts perfect.[23]

Helen Nimmo, another of the first female students at Queen Margaret College, talks of parents of her day studying a prospectus with 'doubtful shakes of the head, as a distant possibility for promising school-girls'. The preparatory classes in Classics and mathematics at the university, she notes, were even more important than the degree classes because of the 'backward state' of education for women:

> Their informality was as striking as their proportions. When I passed through 'Middle Latin,' I was one of seven, who sat round a table in the old Studio, surrounded by models of classical statuary. We knew each other familiarly, and during the interval before the hour struck we made more noise, one lecturer complained, than two hundred men in the Humanity classroom at 'the Hill'. 'You have such shrill voices,' he observed in making his private moan to one of us, 'you make grammatical errors that would be whipped out of a boy before he was twelve, and yet you have more feeling for prose than men far ahead of you.'[24]

But she recounted an incident which demonstrates the willingness of the female students to learn, and an ability to stand up for themselves in the new male-dominated world of higher education in which they found themselves. The example she gave was in a matter involving 'Meal Monday'. This was a traditional holiday observed by universities in Scotland, which was originally a long weekend granted to allow students to travel back to their homes in the country and replenish food supplies:

> It was no very uncommon thing in my day to interrupt a lecturer in mathematics when his progressions had arrived half-way down the second blackboard, and tell him we had lost the thread of his discourse somewhere near the bottom of the first, and would he please make his figures and his reasoning clearer. On one occasion I recollect a junior class had somehow got a lesson behind the corresponding class at the University (I think the Professor had been at a funeral one day,) anyway when the first 'Meal Monday' was intimated, we on our side announced that we had no desire for any such holiday that year, and should feel obliged by the lecturer coming in as usual on Monday, to make up for lost time. He smiled, and did as we desired.[25]

A key figure in the organisation and work of the Glasgow Association for the Higher Education of Women and Queen Margaret College was Janet Galloway, who was one of the secretaries of the association. She continued as Honorary Secretary of the College, before subsequently taking up a role as a university official. Born in Campsie in 1841, she was trained by her father in office work after leaving school.

Galloway is commemorated in a memorial window in Glasgow's Bute Hall along with Isabella Elder and Jessie Campbell. At an address given at the unveiling of the window, her dedication to furthering women's higher education was praised at length:

> Finding by experience the disadvantages to which women were subjected by reason of the restricted character of their education and the consequent limitation of their activities, she became an ardent supporter of the movement for the removal of these limitations and for the provision for women of an education of the same character as that of men.[26]

It is said that Galloway disapproved of women's suffrage.[27] But her activities to further the cause of women's education included travelling abroad to the great exhibition of 1893 in Chicago, where she represented Queen Margaret College and the Higher Education of Women in Glasgow and the west of Scotland. The US exposition was held to celebrate the 400th anniversary of Christopher Columbus and was attended by millions of people over the six months it ran for.

As a university official, the care and attention to her students was said to be unstinting. 'She knew her students personally, she was interested in each of them, she encouraged them, advised them, helped them in their difficulties, visited them when they were sick and, if need be, fought for them.'[28] She also worked to promote an active social life among the students, encouraging the formation of societies in debating and drama, for example.

Jessie Campbell said of her:

From the first Miss Galloway took up her position on the side of the College: she desired for the students all educational possibilities, and wished that the College might gradually learn to govern itself through its higher students...Her work has been purely voluntary; her reward has been in the devotion of the students, whose well-being has been her life-work for her interest in them at home and in all parts of the world never fails.[29]

Queen Margaret College was incorporated into the university in 1892. Two years later Marion Gilchrist, Alice Cumming, Elizabeth Lyness and Margaret Dewar became the first women to graduate in medicine from a Scottish University. The first female graduate in Arts was Isabella Blacklock, who obtained an MA in 1895, while Ruth Pirret became the first BSc graduate three years after that. Breakthroughs in other key areas came much later; the first female law graduate was Madge Anderson in 1919. She also became the first woman to be admitted to the legal profession in the UK. Marion Stewart became the first female veterinary graduate in 1930 and went on to become the first woman to be registered as a vet in Scotland.[30]

During this time, the college also underwent a rapid expansion in numbers, from its initial task of educating 240 students. By 1909, this number had grown to 600 and by the 1930s there were usually around 1,100 female students attending.[31] The endlessly growing student population meant the college eventually became a victim of its own success. The building that Isabella Elder had gifted, which revolutionised women's higher education in Glasgow, was creaking at the seams due to the boom in numbers; so much so, that many female students opted to attend lectures at Glasgow University instead. In 1935, the college was completely wound up and North Park House was sold to the BBC. North Park House still stands to this day, but is more likely to be known to modern generations as the home of the BBC than the first home of women's university education in Glasgow. The broadcaster was based there for seventy years, from 1934 until 2007, when the building changed hands again and became corporate headquarters.

Meanwhile the name of Queen Margaret College lives on the small social club set up for female students which was to become Glasgow University's Queen Margaret Union. It opened its membership to men in 1979.

Thanks to the efforts of Elder, Galloway and Jessie Campbell, and many other pioneers of female higher education, the university doors have been well and truly opened for generations of women following in their footsteps. It took many more years before women were fully represented in university in life – it is widely held that it wasn't until 1940 that Scotland's first female professor was appointed: Margaret Fairlie, who held the post of Professor of Obstetrics and Gynaecology at the Dundee medical college of St Andrews University. She was still the only woman professor upon her retirement in 1956.[32] However, recent research has suggested that the Glasgow Athenaeum School of Music, which is now the Royal Conservatoire of Scotland, made Emma Ritter-Bondy professor of piano in 1892, although the college did not issue degrees at that time.[33] This made her not only the first female professor of a higher education institution in Scotland, but in the UK.

In the nineteenth century, by the time she arrived at the university, Annie McMillan noted that much of the groundwork had been done and she no longer had to 'plead for every class'. But she pointed out that the early years were as much about proving that women wanted, and should have, a place in higher education institutions, as it was about opening up access:

We had to prove to a critical public, sometimes to more critical parents, and, above all, to a critical, a powerful, and a mysterious Senate, that without the stimulus of opposition, without a degree, we existed in sufficient numbers and were imbued with sufficient earnestness to encourage those who had it in their power to extend our privileges. We had to prove that College life did not rank amongst fashionable crazes, or as a remedy for ennui, but that even then, in its restricted sense, it was a real preparation for the wider life lying beyond the College walls.[34]

And when women were accepted into universities, Helen Nimmo pointed out that fellow male students and the public rapidly became used to seeing a 'sprinkling of girlish faces and figures' at graduation capping ceremonies. She sums the significance of the moment up neatly, in words which still ring true today: 'Does not ones' capping; seem after all one of the big events of life, at the time? It means so much work past, and so many possibilities to come.'[35]

CHAPTER TWO

Work: 'The Hopes of Tomorrow'

On the night of 1 November 1889, a severe gale battered Glasgow. Hundreds of girls and women were at work in a factory making carpets to furnish the Victorian homes of the wealthy. Workmen were building a new mill next door, which had an elaborate and distinctive façade modelled on a Venetian Gothic Palace, to appease the wealthy residents in surrounding streets. Shortly after they downed tools and left for the night, the mill building being constructed gave way without warning and crushed twenty-nine female workers to death. The early reports of the disaster at Messrs Templeton & Sons in Binnie Street convey the horror and shock of the night:

> The works at the time were in full operation, and the employees were engaged, as usual, in the sheds and were practically buried in the debris. An alarm was at once raised, and assistance rendered. Altogether up until 9.15 there had been seven bodies taken out. Some of them were mangled to an extent that made them almost unrecognisable. The body of a girl was found to have been decapitated by the falling wall… Owing to the stampede that took place among the workers when the accident occurred it is impossible to say how many bodies are still in the ruins.[1]

Most of the victims were teenagers or in their early twenties, with the youngest aged just 14 years old. There was horror across the city at the disaster and it was the worst peacetime tragedy in the east end. It is an extreme example, but the reality was that while the wealthy were battling to access education, life for many women in Glasgow was one of hard graft as industry boomed. The city was at the centre of the new era of prosperity thanks to a revolution in steel, coal and shipbuilding in the late eighteenth and early nineteenth century, and there was an increasing trend for women's work to be carried out in factories. It was largely the domain of young single women, as the role of women was still very much seen as belonging at home. Many would work until marriage, and then only casually or part-time afterwards, or return to a job if they were deserted by their husband or widowed. The number of women employed in major industries in Glasgow grew from around 100,000 in 1891 to just over 112,000 in 1911. During that time, there was a decrease in work in some professions such as domestic service and an increase in women employed in hotel and 'eating house' services, tailoring, dressmaking and tobacco manufacture.[2]

This workforce of women were no strangers to battling for better pay and working conditions. During the period 1850 to 1914, there were 300 strikes involving Scottish women.[3] A number of official trade union bodies were set up in the closing decades of the nineteenth century, including the Scottish Council for Women's Trades in 1887, from which emerged the Glasgow Council for Women's Trades.[4] The National Federal Council of Scotland for Women's Trades was established in 1893 and when its second annual conference was held in Glasgow in 1895, it was noted that 14 trades' councils and 21 societies representing women workers were now connected with the body, representing 93,526 people.[5] The report detailed some of the work that had been undertaken during the year, including an inquiry into the employment of women in shops. This took evidence from 80 people and found that days of 16 and 17 hours were being worked, with as many as 90 to 100 hours per week in some cases.

Even while the focus was on the issue of women's employment, frustration at the lack of suffrage was never far away, with campaigners pointing out that the two were intricately connected. The question quite rightly raised was how could women have a say in their working conditions when they had no voice at the ballot box? Among the critical voices was leading activist Margaret Irwin, the secretary of the National Federal Council of Scotland for Women's Trades, who pointed out a crucial aspect lacking in the work being carried out to try to improve working conditions was that women could not influence politicians through voting:

> The work during the year had been important and satisfactory. One thing that made the help of men in connection with women's trades necessary was that men had votes. The women, however, meant to have votes of their own someday, but until that day came the next thing was to be able to influence those who had votes, and that they could do by means of their federation. It was not sufficiently recognised that the women's suffrage question was much more a labour question than anything else.

Margaret Irwin, born in 1858, was one of the students who attended Queen Margaret College. She had a distinctive middle name – Hardinge – taken from the unusual start she had in life being born on the *Lord Hardinge* ship, the daughter of a ship's captain. Her influence in the trade union movement was significant, starting off as the secretary of the Women's Protective and Provident League, before taking up a post as the secretary of the Scottish Council for Women's Trades. She campaigned for the setting up of the Scottish Trades Union Congress (STUC) and was elected as its first secretary. She was also a founding member and secretary of the Glasgow and West of Scotland Women's Suffrage Association.

Her mission in life was to improve the conditions for women in the workforce and she carried out investigations into the employment of women workers in several industries, the results of which reveal much about the labour conditions of the time. In 1896, she outlined the findings on women's industries in Scotland collected for the Royal Commission of Labour in an address before the Philosophical Society of Glasgow. She noted:

There is perhaps no centre in the United Kingdom that provides so rich a field for the economic investigator as Glasgow does. It is estimated there are over 300 different industries carried on here, which is a larger variety than is to be found even in London itself.[6]

The key issues which she identified as 'paramount importance' for the social reformer are those which do not sound unfamiliar to the concerns which are still being discussed a century later, that of a 'living wage' and of equal pay.

We hear sometimes of a 'wage that just keeps body and soul together'. To my thinking that usually means the wage best calculated to keep them apart; for if the whole physical power is engaged in a hand-to-hand fight with poverty, I am afraid very little energy can be left for keeping life in the mind or soul. Speaking generally, I have always found that the conduct, health and standard of social and family life among working women is more largely regulated by the *wages* they receive than by anything else. This rule is, of course, subject to modification in individuals, through temperament, training, and other circumstances; but I have no hesitation in stating, as a general principle, that where women's wages are high the standard of conduct, health and family and social life will usually be found to be correspondingly high. When wages are low the reverse is the case…the average working girl usually finds it much easier to be good and amiable on 20s a week than on 5s.

On the issue of equal pay, she noted that there were 5,000 women employed in the tailoring trade in Glasgow, but only three shops where women were being paid the same rates as men for doing the same work. She highlighted some examples of huge gaps in pay:

For instance, when a man makes a dress vest, he may receive 7s 6d for it. When a woman makes the same vest, she gets 3s 6d. For garments for which the man's rate is 3s 6d, the women gets 3s and 1s 6d, sometimes as low as 9d. The result of this is that a rapid displacement of male by female labour is going on in shops of the lower class.

Another example she gave was in factories, where signs stated that the rate for men for cigarette rolling is 1s per 1,000 (the equivalent of around £17 today). But it was also stated that for the same task a woman will be paid 9d (about £13 today). It was a discrepancy, which Irwin noted, that was not being passed on to the consumers who bought the goods:

> Now it seems reasonable to expect that when there are large discrepancies in the wages of the worker, a corresponding difference would be found in the prices charged to the public for the goods made by the respective sexes. So far as I am aware, however, the difference stops short at the pay-books of the worker, and the vest and the cigarette made by the woman has the same value put upon it when it goes into the market as that made by the man. If, however, any gentleman present can inform me of a reduction in his tailor's or tobacconist's bill because of the goods supplied being the product of women's labour, I shall be glad to note the fact for future reference.

Another area of industry involving female workers investigated by Irwin was that of work at home; this was a term used loosely which could either mean work solely undertaken in the house, or extra work taken home to finish after they had spent the day in a place of employment. Professor George Adam Smith, chair of the executive committee of the Scottish Council for Women's Trades noted it was 'only occasionally that an approximate living is earned. For the most part the weekly wages are monstrously small, and the hours of work cruelly long...'[7]

A systematic investigation into the conditions of women's employment in home work was carried out by the Scottish Council for Women's Trades over the course of two years. The lengthy list of trades covered during the inquiry ranged from tailoring and dressmaking to paper bag making and sack sewing, as well as doll's dressmaking and book folding. The evidence was gathered from several hundred workers visited in their own homes, as well as employers and public officials. Some of the cases highlighted in the report collated by Irwin show the appalling conditions under which workers toiled, such as a young woman known only as EB, who lived with her parents:

> She works steadily every day from seven in the morning until nine at night. She can very seldom make as much as 8s a week, and often only 4s, especially with the flannelette shirts which chiefly employ her. She is paid 8d a dozen for making these throughout, including lining them, and doing everything required, except putting on buttons and working the button-holes. Each dozen takes twelve hours with the sewing machine, and the seams of them are so heavy you can't lift your arms to your head at night after a day's work on them. Cotton shirts are paid at 1s 9d a dozen for making them throughout, each dozen taking twenty-one hours; and for the boys' shirts, taking seven hours per dozen, she gets 6d. The thread for the men's shirts costs her 3d, and for the boys' 1 ½ d a dozen. Hire of the machine costs 1s 6d a week, oil 2d a week, needles 1d each and 'you smash a lot with heavy seams'.[8]

Another case highlighted in the same report is that of Mrs C., the wife of a labourer who was the mother of seven children and works as a trouser-finisher. With a husband who was 'unsteady in his habits', she was the main bread-winner for the family along with the eldest daughter who worked in a pottery. The family income was supplemented by taking in two male lodgers. The chaotic conditions in which this household lived are described in the report:

> This household of eleven persons was accommodated in two rooms, both of which were in a very dirty and insanitary state. Here too, the work was lying heaped on the floor and the beds. The former furnished a happy hunting-ground for a large and flourishing brood of cockroaches. The sanitary appliances of the tenement were apparently in a very bad state through the neglect or abuse of the occupants. Stair and passage were alike filthy.

Long hours were common: one female worker in an unidentified profession told how all workers had to take home work in order to earn enough to live on. Their day began at 6 a.m. to work before going into the shop, and then they brought home enough work at night to keep them going until midnight. The living conditions of the home workers were found to be 'extremely filthy', with work being carried out under 'highly insanitary conditions'. Irwin brings to life the sights and smells of these dwellings in a colourful description of the typical attic room of a home worker, often at the top of a five-storey building and reached by going up a 'dismal and dilapidated staircase' infested by rats or 'haunted by that most pitiable of four-footed creatures, the slum cat':

> The landings are found with all manner of stake debris; and the atmosphere is merely a congestion of evil odours. At every storey narrow, grimy passages stretch to the right and left, and on either side of these, close packed, is a row of 'ticketed houses' – i.e. rooms on which the doors have marked on the outside the number of occupants allowed according to police regulations – regulations that are frequently evaded by means of that unknown and highly elastic quantity, the lodger. On every landing there is a water-tap and sink, both the common property of the tenants, and the latter usually emitting frightful effluvia. Probably the sink represents the entire sanitary system of the landing. Armed with a box of matches and a taper, and battling with what seem to be the almost solid smells of the place, one finally reaches the top, and on being admitted finds, perhaps, a room almost destitute of furniture, the work lying on piles on the dirty floor, or doing duty as bed-clothes for a bed-ridden invalid and the members of the family generally.

Irwin also described the frequent use of the 'box' or concealed bed, a common feature of many of the tenements of Glasgow in the nineteenth century. These were recesses for sleeping which would often be found in the kitchen or another room, which were originally enclosed in a cupboard. Legislation introduced in 1900 meant they had to have adequate ventilation and be open from floor to ceiling. Today, the recesses have been converted for other uses in tenements in Glasgow, such as space for kitchens or a bathroom.

Outdoor toilets were also once the norm in tenements and still commonly in use up until as late as the 1970s.

Irwin noted it had been suggested that the box bed was a 'relic of our cave-dwelling ancestors' which served as a wardrobe, a larder, a playground for children and a storage area for general household clutter during the day:

> It is almost impossible to give any adequate idea of the dreary squalor of many of these places, which have to do duty both as home and workshops, and which do not meet the most elementary requirements of either. The rooms themselves are sometimes overcrowded with dirty lumber representing furniture, sometimes almost destitute of furniture of any kind. The bed...has to receive the vests, trousers, shirts and the other garments on which the mother has been working, the unwashed dinner dishes, the ailing baby, or the grandmother as the case may be. It may also have consigned to its friendly shade the person of that member of the family commonly referred to by his better half as 'him there', during periods when circumstances, alas, render a temporary retirement from society advisable. At night the same enclosure may have to accommodate, above and below, the entire members of the family.

The poverty and sparse living conditions which a 'shawl-fringer' was found enduring was another case highlighted. The only furnishings discovered in the room were an old chair, a broken cradle and some empty packing cases: 'The bed was a mere heap of filthy rags in a corner. Here, as in other cases, the deficiency in blanket and bedding would be made up from the work taken in from the warehouse to be done at home.'

The diet of the workers was just as sparse as the places in which they were living – the main feature of dinner was tea, which has 'perhaps stood for an hour or more infusing on the hob', and eaten with dry bread or a bit of toasted cheese or parings of meat. 'Very rarely indeed does one see wholesome soup or porridge in these homes,' Irwin noted. But she also made sure not to apportion any blame for the circumstances in which these families were living, pointing out that a mother with little time and limited space and cleaning supplies found it extremely difficult to keep a home to a high standard.

There was concern about women in other professions too, particularly shop workers. At the National Federal Council of Scotland for Women's Trades meeting, there were worries raised about the serious effects to health stemming from a lack of seats and 'defective sanitation' in many shops. Professor George Adam Smith addressed the conference and pointed out the scale of the workforce – there were at least 40,000 women assistants working in shops in Scotland, including around 15,000 in Glasgow. 'Did the public realise how many women worked in Glasgow from 70 to 96 hours a week – that was to say from 12 to 16 hours every working day – at a very low rate of wages in labours often of extreme fatigue, and frequently under the most insanitary conditions?' he asked the meeting.

He also called attention to the 'overworking and overloading of message girls…which was a very much greater evil than the public had yet realised. The health of many of these girls…had been ruined before they were 16 years of age, not only by having too long hours, but by being sent out to carry heavy burdens that would be intolerable for men and women of older years.'[9]

The conditions in which shop assistants lived and worked was also investigated by Irwin, who in 1901 gave evidence on the issue before a Select Committee of the House of Lords looking at whether shops should be closing earlier. The establishments which were found to have particularly excessive hours included dairies, fruiterers, confectioners, newsagents, tobacconists, restaurants and ice-cream shops. In some cases bakers and drapers also kept open very late. It might seem late night opening of retailers is a modern phenomenon, but the research covered more than 100 shops that opened between the hours of 10 p.m. and midnight. And the employees had to work lengthy hours to cover the opening times. Irwin said the investigation uncovered working as long as 17 hours in one stretch – and in a number of cases the total daily hours added up to between 14 and 16 hours daily. In addition, 80 to 100 hour weeks were common:

A case of a restaurant was reported to me where the hours, usually from 7.30 in the morning to 11 at night – 15 per day and 93 per week – rose occasionally to 96, 99 and 102 per week. This was due to entertainments being given once or twice a week during the winter season and these girls having to be in attendance until two in the morning at these.[10]

The long hours of opening were a concern for some employers, the report noted, but they said they felt obliged to do so because other shops did. In another case uncovered in a bakery shop, a female worker was found to be on duty all day:

Her hours were from 7am to 8pm and till 11 on Saturdays, weekly total 81. She had no short evening in the week, and had to take her meals as best she could in the shop in all the intervals of serving; she was unable to go outside the shop at all. Her predecessor had left seriously ill. She said that her employer was strongly in favour of early closing, but kept open because the others did.[11]

In another baker's shop, six girls were employed who worked from 6.45 a.m. to 8 p.m. during weekdays and to 11.30 p.m. on Saturdays. One said: 'When I get home I just sit down and cry with fatigue.'

There were also major concerns about the working conditions for women in laundries, which was highlighted in 1891 in the House of Commons. An MP described the conditions they were toiling in and spoke of homes where the washing took place in the kitchen, the ironing in the bedroom and drying of clothes in the passageway and over the beds:

The ventilation in these laundries is bad owing to the fact that they are not provided with drying rooms. The laundresses are required to work in a temperature of 100 degrees; at this time of year in a higher temperature. The atmosphere is also impregnated with steam from clothes drying in the same room. The workwomen are often attacked by infectious diseases, the ironers being particularly liable to consumption owing to the overcrowded and ill-ventilated rooms.

On Monday the people work 12 hours, Tuesday 13, Wednesday 14, Thursday and Friday 14, and Saturday 10, making a total of 77. Nine hours are allowed for meals, so that the working hours number 68. In many of the small laundries the work is crowded into four days and, in consequence, the hours worked are 15, 16, and 18 per day.[12]

Insanitary conditions were also to be found in existence in the tailoring and dressmaking industry, according to another inquiry conducted on behalf of the Scottish Council for Women's Trades by Margaret Irwin. The 'pit' shops were of particular concern, usually downstairs rooms with no natural light where both women and men toiled.

'Many of the shops in the Tailoring Trade are in a very insanitary condition. The two classes of shops which present the most serious structural defects are the "pit" shops and the "attic" shops. The former are practically cellars. For the most part of the year there is no natural light in them, and the gas has to be kept burning from morning till night.

'One pit shop which I visited was reached by a dark and precipitous flight of filthy stairs, which I managed to descend safely after lighting a taper. At the bottom was a sort of dark well forming a landing, and on one hand I found a small, dreary, cell-like apartment in which a woman machinist was employed. The light came from a window below the level of the street pavement, and the place contained no heating apparatus.

'The room in which the men worked was on the same level. It was fairly clean and a good size, but as the only means for warming it was the small stove on which the irons were heated, the cold in winter was intense. One of the men here had the appearance of being in an advanced stage of consumption. In the narrow landing adjacent to the machinists' room and opposite that in which the men worked there was a dark lavatory, apparently in a filthy condition as it ventilated a terrible effluvium directly into the workrooms.'[13]

The 'attic' shops offered little better working conditions, even though they were usually located at the top of five or six flights of stairs. 'Being next to the slates, the same difficulty obtains them as in the "pit" shops of maintaining a comfortable temperature,' Irwin noted. 'The workers say, "In summer you faint with heat, and in winter you freeze with cold."'[14]

Irwin was awarded a CBE for her work in 1927 and was described as a 'recognised authority on industrial conditions relating to women' when she died in January 1940 at the age of 61. She was the organising secretary of the former Scottish Council for Women's Trades and Careers throughout the organisation's 44-year history. On top of this, she also managed to run her own business for many years, where, of course, the conditions for workers were of the best standard:

> In the early years of its work, the Council did much for the betterment of women workers, particularly regarding conditions of shop assistants and of women employed in laundries. It was largely through Miss Irwin's activities that the Council initiated and promoted a mass of useful legislation affecting industrial conditions and showing the urgent necessity for reform of housing conditions of women workers in potato lifting, fish curing, and fruit gathering. For many years she ran a fruit farm of her own in Perthshire, where work was carried out under ideal conditions.[15]

The development of a more prominent role for women in public life and a growing concern over conditions of industrial employment for an increasing female workforce saw the appointment of the first women factory inspectors in the late nineteenth century. The profession had been established in the 1830s to enforce a series of labour laws aimed at regulating conditions in factories and mills, ranging from the hours worked to requirements for meal times and protection against disease and accidents.

One of the first women to be appointed by the Home Office was Glasgow-born Mary Paterson, who took up her post in 1893 along with May Abraham, who was based in London. The female inspectors were appointed to investigate issues such as industrial poisoning and disease, asbestos and working conditions in places such as laundries. In one report on an address to the Royal Institute of Public Health Congress in Aberdeen, Mary Paterson addressed the 'foulness of the air' of laundries: 'She did not think the present haphazard way of allowing the worker to choose between foul air and draughts quite solved the workshop ventilation problem.'[16]

Examples of the work undertaken by Paterson included a number of prosecutions under the Factory and Workshops Act in Newcastle upon Tyne, with charges against employers of dressmakers who had continued to work overtime, after they had already worked thirty days' overtime in the course of a year.[17] The factory inspectors also had particular responsibility concerning when women could take time off for childbirth and their return to work. However, their annual salary was £200, which was significantly less than their male counterparts who earned from between £300-£320.[18]

The 'Who's Who' of Glasgow in 1909 includes a listing on Mary Paterson which notes:

> From the first her headquarters have been in Glasgow, and she has been engaged in peripatetic work, chiefly in Scotland and the North of England, but often extending to other parts of the country. In addition to the ordinary routine work of inspection, she is called on to make many special enquiries into the conditions of women's employment in specified industries and their effects upon health, to investigation complaints, and to enforce the provisions of the Truck Acts. Her duties entail travelling over no less than 10,000 miles a year and often considerably more.

It notes some details on her life before she took up the factory inspector role, which suggests she was well-travelled:

> Before 1893, Miss Paterson was a good deal abroad, especially in Italy and in the United States. She accompanied her uncle Dr Henry Muirhead, to America and made a long tour there, visiting Canada, California and the United States. At home she was much interested in social work, and, beginning with charitable undertakings, gradually found her interest centre in industrial questions affecting women and girls.[19]

The 'Who's Who' of Glasgow published in 1909 contains information on nearly 500 notable citizens of the city. Mary Paterson was just one of seven women listed among them. But even though they didn't have the vote, women of Glasgow were concerned with influencing improvement in life for workers and were actively involved in campaigns and official roles to address the conditions under which many toiled.

The scale of the disaster at the Templeton mill led to a public inquiry taking place in December 1889. And the victims of the horrific factory disaster have not been forgotten today by the community of Calton. A somewhat neglected garden – which according to locals was a memorial to the incident – was given a makeover in 2013, with paving stones engraved with the names of the 29 accident victims.[20] They included Annie Wilson, age 14, Elizabeth McMillan, age 15, sisters Elizabeth and Agnes Broadfoot, who were aged 17 and 21. Margaret Arthur, 20, Margaret Blair, 16, Helen Bradley, 21 and Margaret Cassidy, 18. There is Lilias Davittt, 19, Agnes Dickson, 16, Janie Duffie, 20, Janet Gibson, 16, Dinah Gillies, 19, Jean Glass, 20, Sarah Groves, 22, Ellen Wallace, 23, Margaret McCartney, 17, Minnie McGarrigle, 24, Agnes McGregor, 17, Martha Mackie, 20, Rose Ann McMillan, 21, Jeannie Marshall, 22, Jemima Morris, 23, Grace McQullian, 19, Margaret Shields, 22, Elizabeth Sinclair, 25, Mary Ann Stewart, 16, Annie Strathearn, 19 and Mary Turnbull, age 15. At the end of the simple, low-key path, marking the names of those who died, is a plaque which has an inscription dated September 1954, which reads:

"Green buds for the hopes of tomorrow
Fair flowers, for the joy of today
Sweet memory, the fragrance they leave us
As time gently flows on its way."

CHAPTER THREE

Health: 'Smashed Human Lives'

In the 1870s, the average life expectancy for a woman in Glasgow was just 32.6 years old – slightly more than the equivalent figure for men at 30.9 years old.[1] The city, with all the problems associated with urban deprivation and squalor, was particularly badly hit by the cholera epidemics, which swept Scotland from the 1830s and which led to the establishment of dedicated cholera and fever hospitals. Thousands of lives were lost in Glasgow as these diseases hit the city. The number of deaths in one month alone for the city – which had a population of 400,000 at that point – is hard to comprehend today: 'For a third time cholera returned in December 1853 and by the time it disappeared in December 1854 it claimed no fewer than 3,885 victims, the month of August alone being responsible for 1,023 deaths.'[2]

However, attempts to improve living standards were being made. When another outbreak of the cholera returned just over ten years later in 1866, there were only fifty-five deaths recorded in the outbreak on account of the supply of clean water which was now flowing from Loch Katrine to the city. Measures such as the Public Health (Scotland) Act of 1867 were the start of an attempt to improve living standards and reduce the impact of infectious disease. It led to better housing and sanitation and to the general death rate falling towards the end of the nineteenth century. However, tuberculosis and other infectious diseases still accounted for around a third of deaths. The infant mortality rate gradually fell from an average of 170 per 1,000 live births in children under the age of twelve months, in 1855, to 107 in the 1920s.[3] This was indeed a vast improvement, but compared to today's standards still unbelievably high: in 2017, Scotland had an infant mortality rate of just 4.72 per 1,000 live births.[4] Medicine was also making rapid advances with the development of anaesthetics such as chloroform, discovered by Scot, James Simpson, in 1847, and the pioneering of antiseptics during surgery in 1865 by the Scottish doctor, Joseph Lister, who promoted the idea of sterilising instruments and cleaning wounds while at Glasgow Royal Infirmary.

By the turn of the century, public health was looming large in the minds of politicians, triggered by concerns over the recruitment of soldiers. Addressing the House of Lords in 1903, the Earl of Meath noted that 'physical deterioration' was not occurring across all classes. The physical health of the upper and middle classes had improved and the poor were living under better conditions than those of a century or half-century ago. But he said 'physical weakness' in the lower classes was still excessive and far greater than to be found amongst the 'well-to-do'.

According to the Royal Commission on Physical Training in Scotland, nearly 30 per cent of elementary school children in Edinburgh were badly nourished, 19.17 per cent were in poor health, 12.33 per cent were 'mentally dull' and 78 per cent were physically weak or suffering some kind of disease. Out of 30,000 children in Edinburgh, half were found to be suffering from a throat condition and around 40 per cent from some kind of ear problem. In addition, 259 male children out of 299 and 294 females out of 298 were suffering from either afflictions either of the ear or throat. The Earl of Meath told the House of Lords:

> These figures are more alarming as one would imagine that Edinburgh, with its magnificent situation, in close proximity to its splendid Queen's Park and picturesque Arthur's Seat, would produce healthier children than say, the enormous industrial city of Glasgow. If the children of Edinburgh are in this lamentable condition, what must be the condition of those in Glasgow and of some of the more crowded cities of England?[5]

These conditions made Glasgow as susceptible as everywhere else to major outbreaks of the killer diseases of the time. The Spanish flu outbreak of 1918, one of the worst pandemics ever recorded which killed millions around the world, took its toll on the city. One report in July of that year noted:

> What gives the influenza epidemic importance is not only the serious results in many instances, but the fact that the infection is well-nigh world-wide. The opinion of more than one expert that the severity and extent of the malady are due to the exigencies of war seems not unreasonable. So far as Glasgow is concerned the history of the outbreak shows considerable fluctuation when the mortality incidence is considered. From May 4 to May 18, when the first cases were reported, the small number of deaths was comparatively small. Thereafter, up to the beginning of June, they increased to nearly double. Following this, there was a gradual decrease until the beginning of July, when the numbers again began to augment, culminating in 33 deaths last week.[6]

By October of that year, the grip of the flu epidemic had tightened on the city – one report noted 510 deaths caused by the illness had been identified in just one week, compared to 440 for the previous week. It added: 'The medical men are badly handicapped in their fight against the scourge because of the shortage of doctors and the difficulty in diagnosing the disease.'[7] The advice for trying to survive the flu was in some ways similar to that which is still given today, to go to bed at once. A concoction of pine oil, lavender oil and eucalyptus oil, with an addition of a little menthol was also suggested to relieve symptoms.[8]

Prior to the deadly pandemic of 1918, the case of one woman in Glasgow who contracted flu made headlines with a cautionary note for women about how 'Dangers Lurk in Thin Clothing'. The experience of Maggie Stitt, living in Oran Street in Maryhill, was told as follows:

> More than a year ago I was at a picnic in Milngavie, and after a hearty day's enjoyment I, along with the party, set out on the top of an omnibus

for the city. The night got very cold, and as I had not my jacket with me, but had put on a thin blouse instead, I began to feel very chilly, and when I reached home my mother, with anxious face, declared that I was blue...I was thankful to get to my bed. There I lay quite an invalid for a month or two. If I tried to get up I had to be assisted. I was very light in the head and could not trust myself. Walking was such an effort, as I had severe pains down my limbs and my heart was just as if it would stop beating.[9]

The article notes that 'women and girls are more venturesome than men in going about in changeable weather in lighter clothing than is necessary to be on the safe side.' However, much of Maggie Stitt's tale is then concerned with going on to explain the miraculous effects of 'Dr Williams' pink pill for pale people', which are credited with her cure. That leaves the question of whether it is more of a clever advertising promotion than a cautionary tale.

One of the first specialist hospitals founded in Glasgow was the Maternity Hospital – which was originally established in 1834 in Greyfriars Wynd, before moving to St Andrew's Square in 1841. It moved again to Rottenrow in 1860 – which became the nickname for the hospital for generations to come; and where it remained until the building was demolished in 2001. The elegant archways of the portico and an arched entranceway were preserved on the site.

The significant role played by Rottenrow in improving maternity care is highlighted in a report from the Glasgow Corporation Medical Officer of Health in 1928. Statistics for the early years of the hospital were said to be unavailable, but in 1859 there were 944 patient cases and the number of children born alive was 888. By 1926 the number of patients had risen more than eight-fold, with 7,763 cases and 6,099 children born alive. In the 1920s, an average of 6,224 children were being born every year at the hospital. The figures, the report notes, will 'convey to the public some idea of the enormous work carried on by the hospital'.[10]

An insight into the conditions in the city's hospitals in the nineteenth century can be found in a pamphlet – written by an unknown person – on a visit to the Glasgow Hospital for Sick

Children, which was clearly designed to encourage donations. The hospital was opened in 1883 and initially located in Garnethill. It had three wards containing fifty-five cots and two 'pretty little swing cots' for babies. A total of 153 children were treated in its first month of opening and the observations of the unnamed visitor included:

> ...the children, how nice and clean, and even cheerful, most of them look. Their mothers, or guardians for the time being, took away the poor rags which they had on when brought in, and the children are now dressed in little scarlet jackets – the neat uniform of the hospital. The sad thing is to think of the places to which they must return when dismissed. Yet when the mother comes to take away the child she will, as a rule, bring back the poor old clothes, carefully washed and mended, so far as her scanty means enable her to do. She is ashamed to have her child in dirty things after what she has seen in her visits to the hospital.[11]

Some of the heart-rending examples of children being treated there include 3-year-old Bobby, whose perilous state of health – 'if not rescued in time he would have died' – is said to have stemmed from neglect: 'dirt, starvation and the absence of everything necessary for child life'. There is also the example of Frank, a boy of 8 years old, but who does not look more than 5:

> His had also been a case of illness induced by great neglect. When brought to the hospital he was apparently dying and he weighed only 1 stone 11lb – just 5lb more than the child of three years beside whom he is now standing. In six weeks he has, under careful treatment, gained 1 stone 3lb! Another life saved.[12]

Another case cited is that of Innes, an 8-year-old visitor to the hospital who was a former patient, but has now had his life transformed:

> The sanitary inspector found him one bitterly cold day in January in a low den in the East End – evidently very ill – in a place without fire,

his rags not sufficient to cover him, and filthy beyond description. His only chance for life was removal to the hospital; but on admission he was found to be in such a state of exhaustion that it was doubtful if he could survive the night. By very careful treatment, however, he survived through a prolonged attack of acute bronchitis. He left the hospital quite restored – not in the rags in which he was brought, but in his present suits, the gift of a kind lady; and now he has come to see his former companions, who are crowding round him with glad welcome.[13]

One particularly interesting case mentioned is that of a young girl, who it was believed was suffering a condition known as St Vitus's dance – now more commonly referred to as Sydenham's chorea, which causes constant twitching movements in the limbs, face and body. It often follows a sore throat caused by the streptococcus bug and can also be the result of a bout of scarlet or rheumatic fever. But the conclusion of the cause of the case described at the children's hospital, perhaps reflecting attitudes of the day towards women and education, is that it was the result of too much studying:

Standing near is a very interesting-looking girl of ten, who was brought in suffering the complaint known as St Vitus's dance, brought on, poor thing, by overwork at school – not work imposed on her, but originating in her own earnest desire for improvement, and to obtain distinction. She had passed the fourth standard in the Board school, and was trying for the fifth, when her nervous system became affected, and she was seized with this painful complaint. She is better already, and the doctor has every hope that she will, before long, be completely cured.[14]

The booklet also notes the improvement that had been made with the introduction of the Glasgow Hospital for Sick Children, which treated mainly those from the poorest households:

Of the children I have been speaking of today a large proportion came from 'wretched dwellings, reeking with horrible odours,' as

Mr Dickens describes...filthy to such an extent, as the medical officer told us today, that it often seems impossible to get the dirt removed, and where shaving of the head is frequently a necessary expedient in order to get rid of the parasites which have been so long chronic there. No wonder that so many children have been growing up in Glasgow diseased and deformed when Glasgow had no hospital to offer them. No wonder that when this hospital was first projected, 50 per cent of all the deaths in Glasgow were of children under five years. Much of this will be prevented in future if the hospital, with an efficient dispensary, is well supported.[15]

A hospital which was unique to Scotland when it opened its doors in 1885 was the Glasgow Samaritan Hospital for Women. This was exclusively for the medical and surgical treatment of disease 'peculiar to their sex', with a dispensary – or outpatient clinic — providing advice and medicine for those who could not be admitted into the hospital. The constitution of the hospital also states its intention to 'promote the advancement of medical and surgical science with reference to the diseases of women' and to 'educate and train women in the special duties of women's nurses'.[16]

The requirement for such a facility was outlined in the first annual meeting of the hospital, which stated that until its opening, no women's hospital or dispensary existed:

The necessity for a special institution of the kind had long been recognised by local medical practitioners and others acquainted with the widespread but untended sufferings of the respectable poor in the densely populated districts...and it was believed that a special Institution for the treatment of the more serious diseases of women (whose sufferings were the greatest and most neglected), under the management of Physicians, Surgeons, and Nurses specially qualified by experience for the work, would prove an inestimable blessing not only to suffering female humanity in the immediate district, but also to many beyond it whose cases might require and there obtain that special treatment and attention which such an Institution is of necessity best fitted to bestow.[17]

In the first year of the hospital, ending December 1886, there were 185 patients treated as 'outpatients' and 87 patients in the wards, of whom 84 recovered and 3 died. The diseases and illnesses treated included breast and liver cancer, epilepsy and miscarriage.

A newspaper report on the hospital two years after its founding praised its achievements, with 93 operations performed in the second year of its existence, 293 patients in total treated and no deaths recorded: even though most of the surgery required the use of anaesthetics, a field which was still in the early stages of development. 'Thus taking the operations of two years, 190 in all, there has been a mortality of only something like 1.6 – a very remarkable state of matters when we consider the serious character of the diseases treated.'[18]

But the report was also critical of Scotland lagging behind when it came to the setting up of this kind of specialist facility. A similar hospital was also in the early stages of development in Edinburgh around this time, but they had been long established elsewhere in the world:

America is well to the front in this matter. In New York, Brooklyn, Chicago and Baltimore, there are wealthy hospitals for women, and many of the smaller towns as well have special institutions. France, Germany and Italy have also been long awake to the importance of special work in this branch of surgery. London has its Samaritan Hospital, and throughout England there are many institutions of a similar kind. Scotland, it will thus be seen, has a great deal of lee-way to make up. The Glasgow Hospital is admirable as far as it goes, but it does not go far enough.

By the turn of the century, the hospital was expanding rapidly. In the year ending 1899, there were 1,224 patients seen, including 325 who underwent surgery. Twelve deaths were recorded in that year, but three were 'sent in a dying condition' and the death rate remained under 3 per cent. The chairman's report of that year notes that an important element of the hospital was the chance to provide care and respite to the working-class women whose burden of domestic work meant they often 'toiled on unmurmeringly until they dropped':

> All Hospitals – and perhaps this might very specially be said of the Samaritan Hospital – were based on the assumption not only that the patient would find better skill and more close and careful watching under the roof of a hospital than under the roof of their own home, but very specially that the patients would be removed from the turmoil and excitement and continuous coming and going in a little house with a big family, and be introduced into the calm and still peace that the Hospital offered them, If that were true of all patients it was especially true of women. His only little room might be quiet retirement to the man who was accustomed to the bustle of the workshop or the shipbuilding yard, but to the woman who could only lie down – if she lay down at all – in the very centre of her own scene of labour, and see the thread of her own work lost or unsatisfactorily dealt with, it was obvious that rest and retirement for a woman could not be got under her own roof.[19]

Women were also members of staff as well as patients – including Alice McLaren, an assistant anaesthetist and resident house surgeons Agnes Cameron and Jessie McEwan. However, another hospital went one step further, and was not only exclusively for female patients, but was also staffed entirely by women.

This was Redlands Hospital for Women, which was founded in 1902 as Glasgow Women's Private Hospital. It charged a modest fee for its services and described itself as being for female patients who desire to be treated by their own sex – for 'gentlewomen of limited means, those in lodgings, and the wives and daughters of tradesman who cannot be treated in their homes, but who shrink from the publicity of a general Infirmary'.[20] The weekly charge ranged from 15s to £1 1s – but patients were expected to pay as they could afford, with even the lowest rate to be reduced in exceptional circumstances. The hospital, however, was also dependent on private contributions as the fees only covered around half the expenses.

The driving forces behind the hospital included Alice McLaren, who was the first woman in Britain to hold a resident house physician role at Leith General Hospital. She had come to Glasgow to practise general medicine alongside Dr Elizabeth Pace in 1893, who was also instrumental in the setting up of Redlands. Her achievements were noted in *The Vote*, the newspaper of the Women's Freedom League, when she retired:

> An interesting ceremony was recently held in Queen Margaret College, Glasgow, to mark the retirement of Dr Alice McLaren, who has been in active practice [*sic*] in that city for forty years. A presentation was made to her as a token of the affection and esteem in which she is held by all classes of the community. Dr McLaren graduated MB (Lond) with First Class Honours in 1890 and was one of the first five women to obtain the MD degree in 1893. She started a practice in Glasgow soon after qualification, and was a member of the staffs of the Lock Hospital and of the Samaritan Hospital, and was an extra Hon Physician to the Royal Hospital for Sick Children. Her great interest of recent years has been the establishment of the Redlands Hospital for Women, staffed by medical women, and originally founded by her in 1903 as the Glasgow Women's Private Hospital, of which she was gynaecological surgeon, and later medical superintendent.[21]

Redlands remained staffed entirely by women until 1955, and it was eventually closed in 1978. The conditions treated there ranged from tonsillitis and sciatica to cataracts, diabetes, and appendicitis. At an annual meeting of the hospital in 1932, the work of the institution was described as being important in fulfilling a unique need in the city:

> For it had removed a real fear from the minds of many middle-class women who were unable to afford the expenses of a nursing home. The hospital was also unique, for it was an institution for women staffed exclusively by women, and of it they had made a real success.[22]

The report also noted that the number of patients treated during the year was 779, of which 18 cases had been treated for free. It went on:

> It was obvious...that if the hospital was to keep filling its proper sphere it could not stand still, and in this connection a number of forward steps had been taken throughout the year. One of these was taken when two beds were set aside for the treatment of cancer cases by radium, and already six cases had been treated by radium with good results. Another step was the addition of an out-patient department.[23]

In the same year, a bed was unveiled in the hospital specifically for the treatment of eye diseases in recognition of the work of another health pioneer, Dr Marion Gilchrist, who was the first woman to graduate in medicine from Glasgow University.

Born in Bothwell Park in 1864, she was the ophthalmic surgeon at Redlands Hospital for Women, and for around twenty years the assistant ophthalmic surgeon at the Victoria Infirmary. She also became one of the leading figures of the British Medical Association and the first female chair of its Glasgow division. An obituary published in the *Glasgow Herald* after she died in 1952 at the age of 88 – although somewhat short considering her many achievements – notes that during the First World War she carried on 'single-handed' the work of the eye department at the Victoria Infirmary. She was also an active suffragette, at one meeting held in Glasgow's Charing Cross Halls by the Women's Social and Political Union it was reported: 'Dr Marion Gilchrist, who presided, said that women were smashing glass and burning property, not because they liked to commit such acts, but because it was the only way in which they could call attention to smashed human lives.'[24]

She was also among a deputation of prominent suffragists, who met with magistrates to protest at the action of the police after arresting Emmeline Pankhurst at a meeting in Glasgow, a notorious episode in the fight for the vote, which will be detailed in a later chapter.

An interesting aside concerning Dr Gilchrist is that she was involved in a high profile case in 1905 where she was sued for the huge sum of £10,000 in damages along with another Glasgow medic Dr John Carswell. The action was taken against the doctors by a man named William Purves, who worked as a river pilot, for alleged wrongful incarceration in Gartnavel Asylum and wrongfully certifying him as insane. The case was rejected by Lord Pearson, who found he was insane and suffering from 'an attack of sub-acute mania with homicidal tendency'.[25] Eighteen months later, William Purves shot and wounded Dr Carswell outside a Glasgow hospital.

One Glasgow woman was at the forefront of pioneering changes in nursing, which have lasting impact until this day. Rebecca Strong was born in London in 1843, and in 1867 went to Florence Nightingale's training school in St Thomas's Hospital in the city. In the mid-nineteenth century, the extent of education required by nurses was minimal, but the need for a more professional form of training – and larger numbers of nurses – came with advances being made in medicine such as the development of anaesthetics. Strong drew up a scheme for a thorough basic training for nurses, when before they had been expected to pick up what they could from watching doctors at work or attending some sparse lectures.

When Strong was 10 years old and living in London, the Crimean War started. An interview written on the occasion of her 100th birthday in 1943 said:

> She read of the exploits of the heroic band of nurses whose work for the wounded at Scutari had reduced the death rate of soldiers from 420 to 22 per thousand. Perhaps it was then that her ambition to follow in their footsteps took root in her mind.[26]

She married while in her teens and had a baby daughter, but became a widow at the age of 20 and was never to marry again. After both her parents also died she took up her nursing career and was 'inspired by the instructions that Florence Nightingale personally gave her', including becoming the first nurse ever to take a patient's temperature:

She used a thermometer two-feet long and shaped like a shepherd's crook, and she was later severely reprimanded for her audacity. But she performed the feat accurately, and was permitted to go on doing it. Soon other nurses were doing the same. That was the first small reform in a lifetime which was going to be spent defying tradition and convention and waging endless battles against those firmly entrenched in the belief that the sights and sounds and smells of the hospital ward and operating theatre were not for women, except in the most menial capacity.

Strong became matron of Glasgow Royal Infirmary in 1879 and implemented ideas to improve the status of nursing, such as having staff wear uniforms; before the recognition of the role on cleanliness and antiseptics in preventing infections, it had been common for nurses to wear what they liked. At a time when it was perfectly acceptable – indeed expected – that nurses would drink beer on duty, she controversially enforced a 'no drinking' rule. She worked closely with her colleague at the hospital, renowned Scottish surgeon Sir William Macewen, who shared her conviction that a better education for nurses was required. But it almost came to nothing when she resigned to prove a point over the living standards required for nurses, as the report notes:

She still chuckles to think of it. She wanted a proper nurses' home built instead of having the nurses sleeping and living anywhere in the building, most often just off the wards with their population of sick and dying. 'I am afraid,' she said almost apologetically, 'I was a very troublesome woman. As soon as one step was taken I proposed another. But asking for a nurses' home was too much. I was told quite plainly I had gone too far, and as I knew the work could not advance without it I resigned.'[27]

Strong came back in 1891 having won her battle, and the nurses' home was built. She set up a training scheme in association with Macewen, which included ideas which have lasted throughout the years, such as a preliminary entrance exam and a syllabus which included studies in topics such as anatomy, physiology and hygiene. It was a model which was accepted all over the world and helped turn nursing into a respected and specialised profession.

Reflecting on her work, she was modest in speaking about her achievements: 'Nobody was more fully conscious than I that I was only a pioneer, and the work I did would mean nothing at all today except for the way in which it has grown and developed.'[28]

Strong retired from the Royal Infirmary in 1907, but her fascinating life continued with travelling all over the world, including meeting Mussolini, befriending an Italian princess and attending nursing conferences in countries including Finland and Canada. Somewhere in her possession, the interviewer notes, she kept a 'white feather given to her by a Red Indian chief at a jamboree held in her honour at Banff, in the Rocky Mountains'. She was awarded an OBE in 1939.

Strong died in 1944, at the age of 100. She attributed her long life to 'hard work and simple living'.

CHAPTER FOUR

Suffrage: 'I Want my Vote!'

While women were making steps forward in public life, by the turn of the century, there is little doubt that the idea of female suffrage was still viewed by many as outrageous. The fascinating collection of items relating to women's suffrage at Glasgow Women's Library includes a collection of postcards both for and against the idea, with the latter featuring some shocking images. For example, there is the cartoon picture depicting a woman with her tongue through a mangle and the words: 'There's no end to a woman's tongue'. Another disturbing image shows a woman with scissors being held over her tongue and the slogan: 'That ugly mouth, why don't you shut it? If I had your tongue like this I'd cut it!' One postcard depicts a woman with her tongue being nailed to a table with the words 'Peace at Last'.

A furious poem on the front of another postcard shows women in front of the Houses of Parliament and reads:

> This is 'the house' that man built/ and these are a few of the women of note/ who say they want, and they will have the vote/And think that they ought to have Man's support/Even although HE should have to go short/The sly Suffragette/Who is all on the get/And wants all, in THE HOUSE that man built.

In contrast, some of the postcards are distinctly pro-suffrage – there is a striking image of black and white cat against a background of suffragette colours with the message at the bottom reading:

'I want my Vote!' Another has a poem on the front, again referring to Westminster, which reads:

> This is 'THE HOUSE' that man built/And these are the Members who've been sitting late/Coming out arm in arm from a lengthy debate/ Women and men 'neath the shade of Big Ben/In the Year --- well we cannot exactly say when;/But the brave Suffragette very shortly must get/Into 'THE HOUSE' that man built.

Negative attitudes can be seen elsewhere in the anti-suffrage literature of the time. A book called *Women's Suffrage and National Danger* written by Heber Hart, which is also in the Glasgow Women's Library collection, lists in the contents a series of reasons against giving women the vote including that it would 'undermine popular government', 'endanger the Empire' and 'impair the vitality of the race'. It also argues that it would be unnecessary, useless, and finally, perhaps running out of ideas, there is a whole chapter devoted to making the case against women's suffrage as 'Its effects would generally be bad'.

Sir Almroth Wright, a bacteriologist known for his work on vaccines, was another of the voices strongly opposed to women's suffrage. In a pamphlet entitled 'Suffrage Fallacies',[1] he wrote:

> No doctor can ever lose sight of the fact that the mind of a woman is always threatened with danger from the reverberations of her physiological emergencies. It is with such thoughts that the doctor lets his eyes rest upon the militant suffragist. He cannot shut them to the fact that there is mixed up with the women's movement much mental disorder: and he cannot conceal himself the physiological emergencies which lie behind.

He went on to describe different types of militant suffragists as 'sexually embittered women in whom everything has turned into gall and bitterness of heart and hatred of men' and the 'incomplete', who want to convert the world into an 'epicene institution in which man and woman shall everywhere work side by side at the self-same tasks and for the self-same pay. These wishes can never by any possibility be realized [*sic*].'

However, the voices of women were not silent. One notable contributor to advocating for women's rights was Marion Bernstein, a radical feminist poet who was born in London in 1846 and spent most of her life living in Glasgow. She published much of her work in newspapers, but a collection of her poetry was gathered in her only book, *Mirren's Musings,* in 1876. Her views on equality and social justice were ahead of the mood of her time. For example in the poem, *Wanted a Husband,* she challenges the marriage conventions of the time:

> Wanted a husband who doesn't suppose,
> That all earthly employments one feminine knows –
> That she'll scrub, do the cleaning, and cooking, and baking.
> And plain needlework, hats and caps, and dressmaking.
> Do the family washing, yet always look neat.
> Mind the bairns, with a temper unchangeably sweet,
> Be a cheerful companion, whenever desired,
> And contentedly toil day and night, if required.
> Men expecting as much, one may easily see,
> But they're not what is wanted, at least, not by me.

An interesting point to note is that until 1832, women were not explicitly banned from voting until the Great Reform Act of that year, which defined voters as 'male persons'. While the first petition on women's suffrage was presented to Parliament in that same year, other issues such as the right for women to own property – which wasn't achieved until 1882 – also took up the time and energy of the women's rights agenda. In 1867, the first debate on the issue of women's suffrage took place in Parliament when Liberal John Stuart Mill called for its introduction. He argued that the Representation of the People Act, also known as the Reform Act of 1867, which led to a large part of the male working-class population getting the vote for the first time, should be extended to everyone. He proposed an amendment for the word 'man' to be replaced by the word 'person':

I certainly do think that when we come to universal suffrage, as some time or other we probably shall come—if we extend the vote to all men, we should extend it to all women also. So long, however, as you maintain a property qualification, I do not propose to extend the suffrage to any women but those who have the qualification.[2]

The argument he put forward was that while acknowledging the occupations of most women were likely to remain domestic, the notion that this is incompatible with a keen interest in national affairs was 'utterly futile'.

I know there is an obscure feeling—a feeling which is ashamed to express itself openly—as if women had no right to care about anything, except how they may be the most useful and devoted servants of some man. But as I am convinced that there is not a single Member of this House, whose conscience accuses him of so mean a feeling, I may say without offence, that this claim to confiscate the whole existence of one half of the species for the supposed convenience of the other, appears to me, independently of its injustice, particularly silly…The notion of a hard and fast line of separation between women's occupations and men's—of forbidding women to take interest in the things which interest men—belongs to a gone-by state of society which is receding further and further into the past. We talk of political revolutions, but we do not sufficiently attend to the fact that there has taken place around us a silent domestic revolution; women and men are, for the first time in history, really each other's companions.

But his forward-thinking proposal was to no avail. Yet while the amendment failed, the notion of women being enfranchised did not. Women were playing an increasing role in public life and in 1873, Mrs Jane Arthur, of Paisley became the first woman in Scotland to be elected to a School Board. Not only did she win, she was also the most popular choice, winning the most votes with a total of 6,293, nearly 1,400 ahead of the next candidate.[3] In a letter thanking the electors for their support she said:

I feel deeply grateful for your confidence, and shall consider it a privilege, as well as my duty, to devote myself to the carrying out of the objects we are struggling for, vis, a wider knowledge of the laws of health, and the improvement and extension of the education of girls.[4]

In November 1882, in St Andrew's Hall in Glasgow, a demonstration was held in support of the enfranchisement of women. A newspaper report noted: 'The meeting was specially a "women's" one, the only part of the hall to which men were admitted being the balcony, and there were not a score of the sterner sex present in an otherwise crowded meeting.'[5] Another account of the event in the *Christian Leader* describes the address of Miss Jessie Craigen as the speech of the evening for its 'thrilling oratorical power'.

This lady is one of the greatest orators I have ever heard. She gave the impression of being an independent and original thinker, fearless in speaking out her convictions; and some of the passages of her speech might justly be described as logic on fire.

It goes on to describe her sentences as having an 'almost Shakesperean dignity and music'.

In this for example – 'If women are to help men to nobler thoughts, they must think themselves. How can they think if they are not free? There is no thought in slavery.' She contended that political corruption would never be cured until women took an interest in politics; and one of her remarks under this head might have been spoken by Carlyle – 'Our kings of today,' she said, 'are no longer in Windsor and St James's. They are in the counting-house and workshops, and if you go through the streets on a summer evening you may see them at the corners or passing in and out of the doors of the public house with caps on their heads and short pipes in their mouths. But if these kings who are to govern us have not the wisdom, alas, to govern themselves, what is to become of us?'[6]

It is not entirely known where Jessie Craigen came from originally – some reports say she was from London although one newspaper described her as a 'Scotch lady gifted with a clear head'[7] – but she was one of the early passionate voices in the suffrage campaign.

Although women campaigned unsuccessfully to be included in the Third Reform Act, the issue refused to die and women's suffrage remained firmly on the agenda. A more organised approach now began to be taken – the Women's Franchise League was formed in 1889, followed by the National Union of Women's Suffrage Societies (NUWSS) in 1897, which remained committed to non-militant action during the course of the campaign for the vote.

The aims of the NUWSS were outlined in a statement published on the front page of its newspaper which said it is 'a great association of men and women banded together for the single purpose of obtaining Votes for Women' and that the colours of the union were scarlet, white and green.

> Among its members are people of all parties and people of none. The cause that unites them is the cause of Women's Suffrage, and they work for victory by peaceful methods only. They use neither violence nor intimidation, but rely on political pressure and the education of public opinion.[8]

In 1902, the Glasgow and West of Scotland Society for Women's Suffrage was founded. A copy of the original minutes still exists today, carefully preserved in the city's Mitchell Library archives. The hand-written notes, with details recorded of each meeting, are a tangible and fascinating insight into the beginning of an important phase in history – even if perhaps the women involved in the meeting had no clue then as to how it would unfold.

The minute note of the first meeting, dated 19 May 1902 and signed by Martha Frame reads:

> At the kind invitation of Mrs Greig a meeting was held at 18 Lynedoch Crescent on Friday the 2nd May 1902 to consider the question of forming an Association for Women's Suffrage...The Secretary was instructed to draw up a draft Constitution to be submitted to the next meeting of the Provisional Committee. It was agreed that a further

meeting should be held on Monday 19th May 1902 at half past two o'clock within the office of the Scottish Council for Women's Trades, 58 Renfield St.[9]

A year later, there were twenty-four names listed on the Executive Committee including some key founding members, such as Dr Marion Gilchrist, Janie Allan and Margaret Irwin.

A report on the society's annual meeting in 1907 notes that there was a membership of around 600 and the influence and work of the association was steadily growing, although it was noted that perhaps a greater increase would have been expected given the position which the suffrage movement had attained in the past two years. The chairman's address to the meeting suggested a move towards more radical tactics, albeit still peaceful action:

> He thought the time was coming when they would have to do a little more than merely agitate. They were told the greatest force against women getting the franchise was the women themselves. That was his own opinion. They were handicapped in the sending of men to Parliament, but he could not for the life of him see why women worked for men who would not pledge themselves to support Women's Suffrage…His suggestion would be the adoption by the women of the only method that was not criminal, and that was that they should withhold their Imperial taxes until they had some say in administering the law. That was the only legitimate method of breaking the law without becoming a criminal.[10]

One of the founders of the Glasgow and West of Scotland Association for Women's Suffrage, Janie Allan, appeared in court in 1913 for the non-payment of £109 in taxes. Her argument was that because she did not have the right to vote and was not considered a person within the sphere of franchise legislation, to then expect her to pay taxes was a form of 'tyranny' being imposed by the government:

> Speaking quietly from notes, Miss Allan said that she wished to make some observations in support of her defence. She cited an Act of

Edward I, to the effect that no tax was to be imposed without the assent of the representation of those taxed, and declared that in the time of Richard II, women as well as men had the right to go to Parliament or to send representatives there. The Reform Act of 1832 attempted to limit the right to males.

Government rested on the consent of the governed, and that consent women were entitled and justified in refusing until they were enfranchised. She objected to pay the tax because taxation without representation was tyranny...she, while representation was denied to women, must resist taxation imposed by an authority as irresponsible and tyrannical. She maintained that if she were not a person within the meaning of the Franchise Acts, she ought not to be considered a person within the meaning of the Finance Act.[11]

However, the report notes that her arguments were - unsurprisingly given the prevailing attitudes of the day – rejected by the judge Lord Cullen.

In 1903, the Women's Social and Political Union (WSPU) was formed by Emmeline Pankhurst and her daughter Christabel, which was to move towards tactics such as hunger strikes, arson and window-breaking to become the leading militant suffrage organisation in the UK. The Scottish headquarters of the WSPU, sited at 141 Bath Street, was opened in January 1908 by Dr Marion Gilchrist, and Glasgow artist Helen Fraser became the first full-time organiser for the organisation.

Questioning of the leadership of the Pankhursts and their tactics led to the founding of the Women's Freedom League in 1907. In Scotland, this group which, while prepared to break the law, was peaceful, was led by Teresa Billington-Greig, with a centre opened in Gordon Street. One meeting of the society discussed the issue of the press 'turning a blind eye' to the 'abuses which prevailed unchecked in our midst':

Miss C Nina Boyle, the principal, declared that the movement in furtherance of the vote for women was progressing famously, and there was no cause whatever for being down-hearted. The newspapers, she proceeded, could not possibly get on unless they had something or other to say about women. The ladies' dress, for instance, came in for much of the criticism. When the attire was loose-fitting it was 'disgustingly dirty and insanitary', when the skirt was narrow then the critics said it was 'silly'; and when it was slit then the verdict was 'shocking'. Women were always wrong. But the great thing was they were attracting notice.[12]

The suffragette movement has of course become known for militant tactics and hunger strikes, culminating in Emily Wilding Davison's death in front of King George V's horse at the Epsom Derby in 1913, but a range of other peaceful action was also taken. A report in *The Suffragette* magazine in 1913 claims the WSPU played 'no inconsiderable part' in the 'crushing defeat' of the Liberal MP in the South Lanarkshire by-election by addressing meetings, with the skills of Glasgow suffragette Helen Crawfurd particularly praised:

During the whole course of the election our speakers have held crowded and enthusiastic meetings. The interest has never flagged. Practically every town and village in the constituency has been visited, some of them several times. Four splendid meetings in different towns were held on the eve of the polling day by that indefatigable speaker and worker, Mrs Crawfurd. She also spoke on Tuesday in the Public Hall of Crawford. Other equally fine meetings were those addressed by Mrs John at Law and at Chapelton, and by Miss McLean at Coalburn. The last of a series of meetings in Carluke was held in the Town Hall on Tuesday, Miss McLean and Miss Thomson being the speakers. A particularly encouraging meeting was that arranged by Mrs Matheson for the mill girls of the town of Lanark. Mrs Crawfurd was the speaker, and she had a record sale of badges and literature, great interest and sympathy being aroused.

All through the election, indeed, we have had the most perfect sympathy and understanding on the part of the women. Keen, intelligent, and thoroughly up-to-date in political matters, their whole

INTRODUCTION

Above: *A woman voting for the first time in St Rollox, Glasgow. (Source:* Daily Record and Mail*)*

Right: *The Suffragette Oak in Kelvingrove Park, planted in 1918 by Glasgow suffrage societies. (Copyright: Judith Vallely)*

Above left: *Jessie Campbell (Picture reproduced courtesy of Glasgow University Archive Service)*

Above right: *Statue of Isabella Elder in Elder Park, Glasgow. (Copyright: Judith Vallely)*

Left: *Janet Galloway (Picture reproduced courtesy of Glasgow University Archive Service)*

Above: *The ornate façade of Templeton on the Green, formerly known as the Templeton Carpet Factory. (Copyright: Judith Vallely)*

Right: *The simple path inscribed with the names of victims at Templeton Memorial Garden, Calton, Glasgow. (Copyright: Judith Vallely)*

CHAPTER THREE

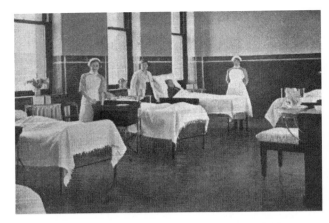

Left: *A ward at Glasgow Royal Maternity Hospital, circa 1920s.*

Below left: *A nursery at Glasgow Royal Maternity Hospital, circa 1920s.*

Below right: *Nurse Rebecca Strong. (Source:* Glasgow Herald*)*

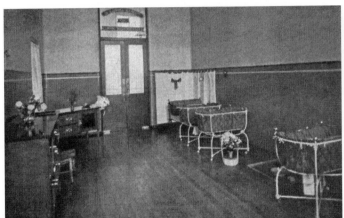

Marion Gilchrist, second left. (Picture reproduced courtesy of Glasgow University Archive Service)

CHAPTER FOUR

Right: *Suffragette postcard from Glasgow Women's Library collection. (Copyright holder unknown)*

Below: *Anti-suffrage postcard from Glasgow Women's Library collection. (Copyright holder unknown)*

I want my Vote!

THAT UGLY MOUTH,
WHY DON'T YOU SHUT IT??
IF I HAD YOUR TONGUE,
LIKE THIS I'D CUT IT!

Left: *Photograph of the suffragette Fanny Parker, alias Janet Arthur, being escorted from Ayr Sheriff Court by a police officer. Miss Parker, a niece of Lord Kitchener, faced trial for attempting to burn Robert Burns' cottage in Alloway. (Crown copyright, National Records of Scotland Ref HH16/43/58)*

Below: *'A novel method of advertising Miss Pankhurst's Glasgow meeting' from Votes for Women' December 16 1910. (Newspaper image © The British Library)*

The aftermath of the attempted bombing at Kibble Palace. (Source: Daily Record and Mail*)*

CHAPTER SIX

Nurse Catherine Carruthers, of the Territorial Nursing Service. (Source: The War Illustrated*)*

Mary Barbour sculpture in Govan, Glasgow depicting her leading rent strikers. (Picture credit: Judith Vallely)

Rent strike demonstration in Glasgow. (Source: Daily Record)

Eunice Murray, the first female MP candidate in Scotland. (Source: Daily Record and Mail)

attitude has been the best possible answer to the excuse put forward by Sir Walter Menzies, the late representative for South Lanarkshire, for his lukewarmness on the question of Woman Suffrage – 'The women of my constituency do not want the vote'. We can safely say, from six weeks' experience amongst them, that there is no country nor shire in the United Kingdom where women are more anxious and more determined to have the vote.[13]

Meetings were held on Glasgow Green and 'self-denial' weeks were arranged in which members of the WSPU went without luxury items to raise funds for the suffrage movement. The suffrage movement also used their publications to highlight injustices faced by women in society, including the attitudes in the judicial system. In *Votes for Women*, the official newspaper of the WSPU, examples were noted in a regular page headlined 'Comparison of Punishments':

The Glasgow Weekly Mail (November 29) reports case of a man charged at Dundee Police Court with assaulting his wife by striking her on the mouth and nose. The reason alleged was that he became suddenly jealous of a guest who had had supper with them, though he had left the house and there was no foundation for suspicion. The Bailie, advising defendant not to invite people to the house of whom he was jealous, *dismissed the case.*[14]

The italics added by the editors of *Votes for Women*, show that such a decision then was just as shocking to some as it would be by today's standards. The regular column highlighted other cases such as:

The Glasgow Evening Times (October 21) reports case of a labourer charged before Bailie James Cairns at Glasgow Southern Police Court with assaulting his wife by smashing a chair over her head. Her loss of blood was so great that she had to be taken to the Infirmary. Sentence: *Twenty days' imprisonment.*

But in comparison with this, there is a case of a heavy sentence involving a domestic servant charged with stealing electroplate dishes, with a value of £1 17s and 6d, and one pound of bacon. She was sentenced to one year's hard labour.[15]

The issue of lack of action to prevent violence against women was highlighted by Janie Allan, citing statistics that two out of three cases heard before a jury at Glasgow Sheriff Court had involved offences 'of a very serious nature' against women and children, with five cases out of fifteen at the High Court also involving such crimes. She raised concerns about the willingness of the Crown to accept pleas of 'attempt', which lessened the punishment.

> Sheriff Lyell last week referred to the 'epidemic of such crimes' in Glasgow, and said it was becoming an 'intolerable scandal'. He thought the adoption of stronger measures in dealing with these cases should be considered and whether such charges should not be dealt with in the High Court.[16]

But the *Votes for Women* editorial notes:

> As long, however, as the disparity of sentences, shown in our weekly Comparison of Punishments, continues to characterise the law courts of this country, we fear this ghastly epidemic of crimes against women and children will not abate. Nothing but raising the status of women by giving her the full right of citizenship, symbolised in the vote, will really go to the root of the matter.[17]

One of the most famous peaceful demonstrations by the suffragists was the first large march organised by the NUWSS on 9th February 1907, in which around 3,000 women took part. The event in London was considered a success, despite wet weather which led to it being dubbed the Mud March.

Scotland had its own version too, when several thousand women – including representatives from Glasgow – took to the streets of Edinburgh in 1909 in a march, albeit organised by the militant WSPU. Unlike the Mud March, this demonstration was favoured by the 'best of weather' and the descriptions suggest it was a lively vibrant affair, with bands, music – including five girl pipers – and a procession on lorries which represented famous Scottish women such as Queen Margaret and Flora Macdonald. A series of banners bore message such as 'We fight to win', and addressing the prime minister – 'To Mr Asquith – you maunna tramp on the Scotch thistle, laddie'. Another read: 'What's good for John is good for Janet'. The march ended in Waverley Market – which had been decorated in the green, white and purple colours of the WSPU – and there was a series of impassioned speeches, including by Emmeline Pethick-Lawrence who told the crowd:

> It was a crusade – a holy war. It was a war not to save a sacred temple from desecration, but a war to save a sacred temple from desecration: that temple was the body and the soul of woman, which so long had lain under the desecration of sex dominance. Death could not kill that which could not die, and there was something which could not die in this movement. Death and victory it might be, but victory it would be in any case.

The report went on: 'Miss Christabel Pankhurst said they were going to make votes for women the issue at the forthcoming London by-election. She defended violence. Nature taught them violence. A thunderstorm brought peace in its train.'[18]

Hostility towards suffragettes was evident when even peaceful action was met with criticism. A march in Glasgow by religious and philanthropic bodies to protest against an extension of publicans' hours of sale – said to be in the name of the poorest women of the city – was reported to have to be abandoned it was claimed: 'As suffragists had made known their intention to join the procession with a view to proclaiming their own cause the city procession was at the last moment abandoned. The citizens are very wroth at the interference of the suffragists.'[19]

Yet it's important to note not all women backed suffrage, or the idea of being entitled to exactly the same rights as men. The minutes of the Glasgow and West of Scotland Association for Women's Suffrage in 1903 noted that a letter had been submitted from a member which stated 'she could not join the Executive of this Association as in her opinion the Franchise ought to be granted to a more limited class of women that this Association demands.'[20]

But the movement received the support of some men. In 1913, a report in *Jus Suffragii*, the official journal of the International Woman Suffrage Alliance, which collated news from suffrage societies around the world, described a group of local officials from Scotland attempting a meeting with the Prime Minister Herbert Henry Asquith:

> In August a deputation of members of Town Councils in Scotland sought an interview with Mr Asquith in order to lay before him the case for Women's Suffrage. The British Prime Minister refused to see them, although he always maintains that he is not provided with evidence that there is any demand for Women's Suffrage. He also declares that the only evidence that he will accept is that of the ballot-box. These Scotch bailies have now formed a league of men to provide this evidence. They are pledged to oppose any political party whose leader does not support votes for women.
>
> 'Scotch Liberals may yet teach the Liberal Government a lesson.'[21]

Although many MPs initially opposed votes for women, another supporter was the founder of the Labour party Keir Hardie, who had strong links with Glasgow. In a 'A plea for Women's Suffrage' in 1905 he wrote of the increasing move towards more forceful and visible demonstrations by women around the General Election of that year, such as creating disturbances at political meetings, and suggesting indeed that it was the way forward:

> The older and more staid Women Suffragists, for the most part, disclaimed all sympathy with these noisy tactics, forgetful of the fact that 36 years of 'tactful' and 'constitutional' work had left little if any mark on the history of the movement. In May this year a few of the ladies of the new movement made a disturbance in the House of Commons whilst a suffrage resolution was under discussion. Mainly as a result of these tactics a very widespread interest is now felt in the question. The present House of Commons is, I think, overwhelmingly

in favour of granting the suffrage to women, but they must not leave anything to chance or take anything for granted.

A big sustained agitation, would, I feel assured, result in securing the passage of an enfranchising Bill in time to enable women to vote at the next General Election. For the second time success is within their reach if only women will not be content to be put off by fine words and sympathetic professions. These are all very well in their way, but they are a poor substitute for an Act of Parliament.[22]

There was indeed sustained agitation and violent tactics; including by women of Glasgow.

CHAPTER FIVE

Suffragettes: 'Fighting for my Liberty'

The adoption of militant methods in the campaign for the vote led to a new word entering the language, one which is familiar to us today, 'suffragette'. Originally coined by the *Daily Mail* newspaper[1] in an article ridiculing the WSPU as distinctive from the peaceful suffragist movement which had gone before it, it was defiantly adopted by the members of the movement who backed taking direct action to win the vote. The suffragettes' motto was famously 'deeds not words'. In Glasgow, there were a number of examples of women who did exactly this to further their cause.

In 1909, for example, plans were hatched to stage a protest on the roof of the old St Andrew's Halls, which had a renowned ballroom and was once a hive of meetings and concerts in the west end. It was destroyed by fire in 1962, but the remaining distinctive façade was incorporated into an extension of the Mitchell Library, which still stands as the entrance on Granville Street today. The daring plot of the suffragettes was to disrupt a political speech by the Liberal politician Robert Crewe-Milnes, the Earl of Crewe, in support of the Budget. But it was thwarted when some alert workmen noticed two planks of wood which they believed had been used to break into the halls. A search of the building was subsequently undertaken, where a young woman was found sitting near one of the ventilation shafts in the large hall:

She was in a woefully chilled and drenched condition, and it was quite evident that the lady had occupied her lofty position during the rainstorm which prevailed in the early hours of the morning. On being questioned, she stated that she had got on to the roof of the halls about one o'clock in the morning, with the intention of remaining there until the Earl of Crewe addressed the meeting in the evening, when she hoped to be able to bring the claims of the women to the franchise under his Lordship's notice. Being further interrogated as to how she had succeeded in reaching the roof of the halls, the lady, it is stated, explained that she had first gained access to the roof of the corridor by scaling planks taken from the adjoining building in course of erection, and by a further manipulation of the same planks had been enabled to get onto the roof of the halls. Her enterprise, she admitted, had been a daring and dangerous one, but she expressed great regret that her attempt to bring the claims of the women before Lord Crewe had failed.[2]

The woman in question was Alice Paul, an American suffragist, who the report went on to say was allowed to leave the building and advised to 'change into dry clothing, and partake of a warm breakfast'. Her fellow campaigners were undaunted by the disruption to the plans, as a number arrived in the afternoon to paint the motto 'Votes for Women' on the pavements surrounding the halls. All were taken to the police station, but allowed to go on; on the condition they ceased the painting.

In the same year, 1909, imprisoned suffragettes began hunger strikes as a form of protest to demand that they should be recognised as political prisoners. In the archives of Glasgow's Mitchell Library is a pamphlet written by Victor Duval, who founded the Men's Political Union for Women's Enfranchisement. It states that the organisation had a growing membership and that thousands of men had enrolled into the Men's League for Women's Suffrage. He noted that while fourteen women suffrage bills had been introduced in Parliament since 1870, only six had passed into a second reading:

> Those who criticise the Suffragists for adopting forcible tactics, and
> say their Cause has been put back owing to these acts of violence,
> would do well to search their own hearts and find what assistance
> they have given to enable women to attain their object in a peaceful
> manner. It is easy for those who enjoy the privilege of deciding what
> laws shall govern them, to dictate to a disenfranchised sex. If men who
> possess the parliamentary vote today, had had to fight for it as their
> forefathers did, then perhaps they would understand the spirit which
> moves women to strong and determined action.[3]

Duval goes on to note that during each month of the year 1909
women were in prison for demanding the vote, with the number
of arrests totalling 294. The number of imprisonments was 163.
In 110 cases, he notes, hunger strike was carried out and in 36
of these, 'the barbarity of forcible feeding was practised by the
government'.

He added: 'The aggregate sentences served during the year by
members of the WSPU was over eight years, bringing the total since
the commencement of the agitation to nearly twenty-eight years in all!'

Suffragettes who endured force feeding in Scottish prisons
included Frances Gordon, who was sentenced at Glasgow High
Court to one year in jail for attempting to set fire to Springhall
House in Rutherglen. After being transferred from Glasgow to
Perth prison, she went on hunger strike and was then force fed.
In July 1914, she was released and sent to a nursing home in an
'exhausted condition'.[4] An account of her brutal treatment was
documented in Sylvia Pankhurst's autobiography, which tells how
Gordon was force fed by tube for a number of days and when she
was released the doctor who attended her described her as looking
like a 'famine victim'.[5]

Another suffragette involved in militant action was New Zealand-
born Janet Arthur, also known as Fanny or Frances Parker, who
became WSPU organiser in the West of Scotland and was involved
in activities in Glasgow and the surrounding areas. A niece of Lord
Kitchener, on one occasion she confronted Winston Churchill,
who at that stage was a member of Prime Minister Herbert Henry

Asquith's cabinet, as he travelled by train between Stranraer and Glasgow on the way back from a visit to Ireland, where he had been confronted by suffragettes. Frances, along with fellow suffragette Ellison Gibson, took up seats in a compartment next to him and quietly waited for an opportunity to speak to him:

> Mr Churchill came boldly along and glared at the two women while speaking to another woman belonging to his party, who had come in beside them. Miss Parker then asked if she might speak to him. 'What on,' he barked. 'On Votes for Women.' 'No, I have had enough of that,' he replied. Asked what the Government was going to do for women, he said. 'For this behaviour you will not get the vote now,' and walked on.[6]

Later, the suffragettes also attempted to confront Churchill as he left his hotel in Glasgow. One WSPU member, Annie Rhoda Greig, was arrested after striking the window of his car with her muff – a popular hand-warmer fashion accessory of the time – and breaking it. Frances Parker also 'made a dash forward to meet Mr Churchill's car', but was held back by a policeman.[7]

The most notorious incident that Frances Parker was linked to was the attempt to blow up Burns' cottage in Alloway, the birthplace of the national poet, in July 1914, which was reported with outrage by the national press:

> A dastardly attempt was made yesterday by Suffragettes to destroy the birthplace of the poet Burns. Explosives were actually placed against the wall of the famous thatched cottage at Alloway, and the fuse attached was just on the point of being lighted, when, fortunately, the perpetrators were surprised by the night watchman.
>
> There were two women, garbed in tight-fitting trousers, and with their skirts tucked up to their waists. They immediately made off, leaving the bombs behind them. The watchman gave chase, and succeeded in catching hold of both of them. One, however, during an exciting struggle, succeeded in breaking away; the other was secured and held prisoner until the arrival of the police.[8]

The woman who was caught was said to have given her name as Janet Arthur, but the reports of the time say that this was believed to be fictitious. One local who lived near the cottage told of her reaction while she was being held:

> When I came up the woman was lying on the ground. She looked like a young man. She was wearing tight trousers, and had drawn her skirt and waterproof up to her waist. She had stockings pulled over her boot....She struggled at first, but afterwards talked a great deal...Men in Scotland, she said, had found their liberty, and the women were only fighting for theirs.[9]

When she appeared at Ayr Sheriff Court, the report said she 'talked continuously', taking no heed of court officials, and raised the issue of force feeding of hunger strikers: 'She complained of the treatment meted out to women in Perth prison, quoted lines from "Scots Wha Hae", relating to liberty, and said that Scotsmen used to be proud of Bruce but had now taken to torturing women.'[10]

Parker was taken to Ayr prison initially but after six days of a hunger and thirst strike she was transferred to Perth prison, where according to Sylvia Pankhurst's autobiography she had to endure brutal treatment, being fed by tube with 'unnecessary violence' and being slapped in the face by a wardress. She was also said to have been held down during the process of force feeding and even lost consciousness after one session.[11]

The suffragettes in Glasgow also travelled to be with their counterparts in other areas of the country to take part in action. For example, a Maggie Moffat from Glasgow was among thirty-four women arrested after taking part in a 'determined raid' on the House of Commons in February 1907, involving several hundred women. The demonstrators tried to 'storm' the building from 4.30 p.m. to 7.30 p.m., with chaotic and violent scenes as police tried to stop them:

> Breaking into one of their songs, the women rushed against the wall of bluecoats, and within the next few minutes a dozen more were in custody. The police did not adopt kid-glove methods, nor did they

try a policy of peaceful persuasion. The encounters were of the most violent nature. Both men and women lost their tempers, and some of the women were roughly handled. Nor did they accept the treatment quietly. Umbrellas were freely used as weapons of attack, and one was broken over a policeman's head. Others kicked wildly. For the most part they rushed in twos and threes. Some of those who had individual tussles fared worse, and were thrown in the mud.[12]

In 1912, Scottish suffragettes took part in window smashing campaigns in London, and as a result received sentences ranging from one to six months' hard labour in Holloway prison. Among them was Helen Crawfurd, who was sentenced for one month[13]. The Glasgow-born minister's wife spent multiple stints in prison for suffragette activities, and later went on to play a prominent role in the Glasgow women's rent strike campaign in 1915, of which more in chapter seven.

Two years later, Glasgow suffragettes were part of a deputation which went to Buckingham Palace to demand votes for women and protest against torture, which was met with police who 'brutally ill-treated the women'. It resulted in the arrest of around sixty women:

Never before within living memory has there been such a scene at a royal palace. All the gates were closed, and within the courtyard were soldiers with bayonets fixed doing sentry duty. Police reserves were there too, to repel attackers if required. Outside were more soldiers and a force of 1,500 policemen on either side of the carriage way. Surrounding the police was a crowd estimated at between 20,000 and 30,000 persons, who had formed up in Constitution Hill, the Mall, and Buckingham Palace Yard.[14]

When the women tried to force the gates, accounts say that they were knocked down by mounted policemen and struck by truncheons. One woman in her invalid chair was 'brutally ill-treated' and had her chair broken up by police.

Among the women involved in that deputation was Janie Allan. Her account of the event published in *The Suffragette* told of 'great roughness and brutality' shown by the police to those arrested. 'They pummelled the women and a man supporter unmercifully, and threw them about in a savage fashion, even after they had been taken into the station room,' she wrote.

> The women broke windows, the glass of pictures and anything they could lay their hands on, but that was no excuse for treating them in such a manner.
>
> One constable said to a woman who attempted to go out of the door, being uncertain if she were under arrest or detained, 'I'll have the nose off your face if you move another step.' Many of the women had terrible bruises, and one Scottish woman whose arms were severely bruised told me that even at Cannon Row Police Station the policeman pinched her arm most vindictively saying: 'That is for what you did in the Park.'[15]

In Glasgow, incidents linked to suffragette action were taking place on a regular basis, including acid attacks on post boxes. For example, in February 1913 a brown paper parcel was discovered by a postal worker in a pillar box at Charing Cross Post Office in Woodside Crescent, Glasgow. It contained a piece of cloth saturated with acid. 'The acid, which was of an inflammable nature, had burned through the paper, and damaged a number of letters.' it was reported.[16] Another similar attack in June of the same year was described:

> A further series of outrages on pillar boxes was discovered in Glasgow last night. The districts in which they took place are the western and southern. In all, five cases were reported to the police. In each case a liquid substance of a corrosive character had been poured into the pillar-box, and in one case the postman who was collecting the letters had his fingers slightly burned. Only a few of the letters were damaged, and none was indecipherable.[17]

Another form of attack aimed at disrupting communications was wire-cutting, such as one incident in which around fifty telegraph and telephone wires were cut in Kilmarnock in the Dunlop and Fenwick areas:

> Cards bearing the words 'Votes for Women' were found at the scene of the outrage. The damage caused considerable delay and inconvenience, but repairs were carried out late in the day. The wires in both cases run alongside the main Glasgow roads, but the places chosen by the suffragettes for their operations are in somewhat remote parts and they were not observed by anyone.[18]

In December 1912, the WSPU shop in Sauchiehall Street in Glasgow was wrecked by some male students, with the incident reported as being triggered by suffragettes heckling a speech by cabinet minister Augustine Birrell, the rector of Glasgow University. While some headlines spoke of 'Tables Turned', *The Suffragette* newspaper's take on the incident was scathing:

> Angry that women, who have forced upon them a war against the long odds of ignorance and tyranny, had questioned Mr Birrell upon the occasion of his Rectorial Address to the students of Glasgow University, a body of these illogical young ruffians marched to the headquarters of the WSPU in Glasgow, and proceeded to wreck the premises. There was, as is so often the hooliganism of the enfranchised male, no reason in their attack, the women simply having attended the meeting, presided over by a Cabinet Minister, in the pursuance of their well-known policy of reminding these official gentry, wherever they are to be found, of their political duty to those women of the country who demand a political status.[19]

One student, John Kirkpatrick, was charged with taking part in disorderly proceedings following the attack, which was described by a witness at the trial as follows:

> She said there were about 200 students, who arrived at the premises a little after midday. First of all the youths smashed in the window, and then broke the glass panels in the door. Swarming in through

the door, they shouted to Miss Christie to clear out and went on smashing furniture. Witnesses spoke to a flag, the familiar tricolour of Suffragettes – purple, white, and green – which was produced in Court, as having been taken from their premises.[20]

In January 1914, the iconic Kibble Palace in Glasgow's Botanic Gardens became the target of a bomb attack. One explosion shattered a number of windows in the glass palace, which had opened in 1873 in Glasgow. It was reported as a 'Bomb Outrage' in various newspapers, including the *Daily Record*:

> Evidence clearly indicates that this was the work of militant Suffragettes, whose plans had been well laid. They would have been successful but for the presence of mind and prompt action of the night attendant Mr David Watters, whose duty it is to attend to the fires. As it was, however, one bomb exploded and seriously damaged the large winter garden, and shattering twenty-seven large panes of glass.[21]

The report tells how the night attendant had observed a piece of burning string, before realising it was attached to a bomb. He cut the burning end off, but after walking a short distance another bomb went off, with the explosion 'heard over a wide area'. After a search the police surmised it was the work of women after discovering footprints of ladies shoes…and an empty champagne bottle and cake:

> In the course of their search the police found numerous footprints on the ground which had been rendered soft by a drizzling rain. Near to the spot where the explosion occurred were found together a lady's black silk veil, a piece of white cotton cloth, and a portion of a Glasgow newspaper…in which, it is believed, the bombs were carried.
>
> Continuing their search, the officers, who were assisted by Mr James Rorke, the manager of the Botanic Gardens, whose residence is within twenty-five yards of the Kibble Palace, discovered that the visitors had partaken of refreshments during their vigil. Pieces of cake and an empty champagne bottle were recovered from the shrubbery immediately adjoining the footprints leading to the Palace.

The Gardens were closed to the public at five o'clock on Friday night, and it is surmised that the women hid themselves until after the closing hour, and then took refuge in one of the greenhouses. The footprints clearly indicate the high heels of ladies shoes.[22]

The tactics of the suffragettes included attacks on high-profile artworks. One of the most notorious incidents was the slashing of a painting in London's National Gallery. Mary Richardson said that she had attacked the *Rokeby Venus* to protest against the arrest of Emmeline Pankhurst but also in protest at men 'gaping' at the nude, by Spanish artist Diego Velazquez. In Glasgow, an attack was also reported at Glasgow Corporation Art Galleries:

The glass was smashed in a large work, 'Head of an Angel', by Corregio. Beneath the picture lay a new hammer, the handle draped with a white satin ribbon. A large number of lady visitors had been observed in the galleries prior to the discovery, but no trace has been obtained of the person who committed the outrage. Two blows had been struck, completely smashing the glass.[23]

In May 1914, an apparent attempt to wreck the main pipe carrying water from Loch Katrine to Glasgow was also blamed on militant suffragists. Two bombs and a half-burned fuse were found on the water main a short distance from Balfron Railway Station, according to a newspaper report:

Near the spot were found two hand trowels, a lady's handbag, a copy of Friday's issue of the journal of the Women's Social and Political Union, and a label bearing the words: 'A protest against the Magistrate's decision not to inquire onto the arrest of Mrs Pankhurst'.

The opinion is held in some quarters that the object of those who placed the bombs was to create alarm without causing damage. But although there was apparently some defects in the fuse, the bombs were not of the harmless description which have been occasionally used in suffragist exploits. On the contrary, they were of deadly construction, investigation showing that each contained half a pound of gelatine. Their explosion would obviously have had serious consequences.[24]

The report notes that the fuse was about 80 feet in length, and had burned out half-way by the time it was discovered. Another surmises that half of Glasgow's water supply would have been cut off, if the attack had been successful. [25]

The arrest to which the note referred was one which took place following a visit by Emmeline Pankhurst to Glasgow in March 1914 to a meeting arranged by the WSPU. She attended to address a large crowd, despite knowing she was at risk of being arrested under the 'Cat and Mouse Act', which allowed for weakened prisoners on hunger strike to be released and then rearrested once their health improved.

The meeting ended in chaotic scenes and the *Daily Record* reported the event with a series of headlines: 'Wild riot in Glasgow; 'Police storm the platform; Women's Stubborn Fight; Revolver shots in St Andrew's Halls; Several Persons injured'.[26] Mrs Pankhurst had entered the hall by one of the main entrances wearing a 'large picture hat with a yellow feather and trimmings and a thick black veil'. After she addressed the crowd of around 5,000 from the platform, uniformed police officers and detectives arrived at the meeting, resulting in uproar:

> Several women who had been seated in the front row of the audience in the area rose up to bar the progress of the police, who were now streaming through the doorway. But the policemen, tolerating no obstruction, pushed the women back, upset the Press tables which had been precipitately vacated, and drew up in a line with batons drawn across the hall.
>
> A combined rush was made to scale the platform, but the excited occupants offered the resistance of violence. The weapons of defence were various, women suddenly crushed to the front wielding Indian clubs. Simultaneously the flower pots fringing the platform were thrown in the faces of the attackers.
>
> Then a resourceful woman, observing that Inspector Walker had almost gained a foothold on the platform, picked up a chair and rammed one of the legs against his face. Fortunately it caught him on the forehead and not in the eye.

> The operations of the women were diverted by bodies of policemen, who forced their way on to the platform by the two side entrances.

According to the report, one woman then fired a revolver several times. Mrs Pankhurst was seized by the police amid great resistance:

> It was only with the greatest difficulty that, amid a screaming and struggling melee, they carried their prisoner down the stair and out of the building. A motor-car was in waiting, and with considerable difficulty Mrs Pankhurst, who seemed in a half-fainting condition, was half carried, half dragged into it.
>
> Among the crowd who offered resistance in the street when Mrs Pankhurst was being carried to the car were several men. One of them, a young lad, struck a constable and knocked him down. He was arrested and taken to the Western Police Office...Even after the disappearance of Mrs Pankhurst pandemonium reigned in the hall. Several women were hysterical, shouting incoherently.[27]

This triggered protests and demands for an inquiry. A 'large and influential' body of Glasgow citizens travelled to London to meet with Scottish MPs and raise their concerns, while a deputation of fourteen women met with magistrates in Glasgow to voice their anger at the conduct of the police at the arrest of Mrs Pankhurst. [28]

Janie Allan gave a statement to the magistrates which denounced the actions of the police, including rushing towards the platform with their batons already drawn to strike 'many unoffending women' and failing to call on Mrs Pankhurst to surrender. One of the speakers was 'seized from behind and received a heavy blow on her right shoulder from a policeman's baton, while another was knocked down and received several severe blows from a baton'. Allan went on:

> We do not deny that many women did undoubtedly do their best to protect Mrs Pankhurst and to prevent her arrest, but we wish to point out that, if the women were obstructing the police in the performance of their duty, the proper course for the police was to arrest them.

She added:

> I should like to mention one other instance of disgraceful and
> inexcusable brutality on the part of the police, which took place in one
> of the passages. Mrs Nixon, a middle-aged women, saw Mrs Pankhurst
> being dragged along the passage in a very brutal way. There were no
> other women about and there were scores of policemen. She rushed
> forward, caught the arm of one of the policemen, and said: 'For
> God's sake, don't do that!' She was immediately felled to the ground
> by a violent blow on the head from a baton. She fell in front of the
> policemen, one of whom then kicked her to the foot of the steps on
> which they were standing and her head was trampled on as they passed
> over her body.

Two women had to receive medical attention following the incident
and one man was arrested. Mrs Pankhurst herself was taken to
the cells of the Central Police Office, and the report noted the
actions of the police in Glasgow had come from an order from
Scotland Yard.

The incident caused a storm of uproar in the city and led to calls
for an inquiry into the incident. *The Suffragette* reported that a 'large
and influential body of Glasgow citizens journeyed to London' to
meet with Scottish MPs, who agreed that a probe should take place.
It also added that 100 new members had signed up to the WSPU
following the event. [29]

A deputation of fourteen women including prominent
campaigners such as Dr Marion Gilchrist, Miss Irwin, and
Miss Maclean also met with Glasgow magistrates to demand
an investigation. A statement given by Janie Allan said that they
wanted to protest against the 'brutal behaviour of the police at
St Andrew's Hall':

> The first point they wished to impress upon them was the fact that
> the policemen rushed upon the platform with their batons already
> drawn. They did not say for what purpose they had come. They did
> not call upon Mrs Pankhurst to surrender. They simply rushed upon

the platform and began to lay about them, striking many unoffending women with their batons. Miss Barbara Wylie, one of the speakers, was seized from behind and received a heavy blow on her right shoulder from a policeman's baton. Mrs Boyd, daughter of the late Bailie M'Lennan, was knocked down and received several severe blows from a baton. They could all bear witness to seeing women attacked in this way.

'We do not deny,' she proceeded 'that many women did undoubtedly do their best to protect Mrs Pankhurst and to prevent her arrest, but we wish to point out that, if the women were obstructing the police in the performance of their duty, the proper course for the police was to arrest them. Mrs Wilson, who is here today, was thrown bodily off the platform.'[30]

The same edition of *The Suffragette* also reports that a protest meeting was held in the city's Cathedral Square with speeches, which ended with 'three ringing cheers for Mrs Pankhurst'[31]. And an editorial in the *Glasgow Herald* also criticised the police for their handling of the situation:

Our correspondence columns of yesterday and today offer the most copious evidence of the widespread feeling of disgust and indignation around by the mishandling, by the Glasgow police authorities, in conjunction with men from Scotland Yard, of a task which ought to have been carried through in such a way as to avoid a riot in a public hall and the use of violent tactics.

Assuming, for the sake of argument, that it was considered advisable to prevent Mrs Pankhurst from addressing this meeting, why was she not arrested before reaching it – and preferably before leaving London? If she eluded the police there, and again at this end of her journey, and again at the entrance to the hall, then the police methods of keeping in touch with conspicuous people who are 'wanted' are surely insufficient to a discreditable and ridiculous degree…The point which we desire to make here is that the collaboration of our police in this stupid enterprise, of Metropolitan origin, was a blunder from first to last.

The protest against the treatment of Mrs Pankhurst throughout the suffragette campaign also took the form of burning down a mansion house in Stewarton in March 1913, with a postcard in the window bearing the words 'Release Mrs Pankhurst'. 'What will the next outrage be?' asked the newspaper headlines of the day.[32]

Another notorious attack on a building took place in July 1913 when Elizabeth Chalmers Smith, one of Scotland's first female medical graduates and the respectable wife of a Reverend, was caught along with fellow WSPU activist Ethel Moorhead trying to burn down an empty property at 6 Park Gardens in the west end of Glasgow. Both women were subsequently sentenced to eight months in prison. After going on hunger strike, Smith became subject to the Cat and Mouse Act, which had been introduced in that year.

However, she succeeded in escaping the law after being released from Duke Street prison under the new legislation. In November she had been confined to a house which was being watched day and night by three plain clothes policemen:

> The manner in which Mrs Smith made good her escape, although by no means original, was exceedingly ingenious and effective. It appears that on Thursday afternoon, just about the time when callers may be expected for 'afternoon tea', a private motor drove up and two ladies stepped out and, after instructing the chauffeur to wait, entered the house.
>
> Both ladies, one of whom was an elderly woman, are well-known Glasgow suffragettes and had called frequently on previous occasions to enquire after Mrs Smith's health.
>
> After a short visit the ladies returned to the motor, but in the meantime a quick change had taken place, and the elderly lady who leant upon the younger woman's arm, was on this occasion Mrs W Chalmers Smith. They hurriedly entered the motor and drove away quickly.

Too late, it seems, the watching policemen realised the deception. 'The trick was cleverly played,' the report went on, '...and the change of dress was highly successful, but one of the detectives had his suspicions aroused, and just as the motor dashed away he made an unsuccessful effort to hold it up. The three watching policemen have since been withdrawn.'[33]

Eight months later brought the outbreak of war in Europe. The campaign of militancy by the suffragettes came to an end, as women turned to supporting the war effort. With it the perceptions of the role of women in British society were finally about to undergo radical change.

CHAPTER SIX

War and Work: 'An Army of Women'

The activities of both the suffragette and peaceful suffragist organisations were suspended as Europe plunged into war in 1914. Many turned their attention instead to urging women to do their bit to support the country. The official magazine of the International Woman Suffrage Alliance noted the contribution being made by women, including that driven by the efforts of suffrage societies:

> 'Your country needs you. Now is the time to show what you can do'. Such are the appeals of war-time, accompanied by appropriate illustration, which call to the men of Britain from each blank wall and hoarding. But to the women of Britain there is no national appeal for help. No official posters picture for them their field of service, and no Government recruiting sergeant points their way to duty. But in truth there is no need for the women of Britain came to her aid at the first echo of the thunders of battle. Even during those black hours of the first week of the war hundreds of women met and organised themselves into an army of social workers – efficient, energetic, dauntless, originating plans of action, dovetailing workers into work, reshaping the Gargantuan pattern of the social fabric.[1]

Some of the tasks undertaken by various suffrage societies included opening workshops for unemployed women, organising the making of toys and 'fireless' cookers, and providing interpreters for hospitals and refugee depots. So much work was undertaken that it was said it was impossible to keep a complete record of activities.

The variety of work can be seen in one account which details the tasks which had been carried out by the Glasgow Society for Women's Suffrage since the war began. This included a setting up of an exchange for voluntary workers, which supplied volunteers in response to requests, such as for canteen workers in munitions factories in Glasgow. An appeal letter sent out from the exchange also resulted in more than 3,000 sandbags being sent for troops. And the work of the 'Cheer Up Clubs for Soldiers' and Sailors Wives' is also described: 'These clubs, inaugurated by the Glasgow Society, have proved a great success, the women who attend them constantly saying how much the clubs have done to cheer and help them through the lonely days.'[2]

The organised effort by women, it was claimed, was the result of the 'long years of educative work of the Women's Movement.':

> For when the history of the Great War comes to be written, it must be recorded that in Great Britain the first active steps for the organisation of war relief work among women were those taken by the Suffrage Societies…Before any Government Department had approved official schemes, before national assistance had been offered to the wives of soldiers called at a moment's notice from the workshop to the camp, before authoritative effort had secured the registration of Belgian refugees, the women of Great Britain, and notably, the Suffragist women, came forward unrecruited and uninvited, ready to work with organised skill at new and essential tasks.[3]

However, acceptance of the new role of women in society was far from instantaneous. A memo was submitted to the prime minister in 1915 by the Women's Interests committee of the National Union of Women's Suffrage Societies (NUWSS), a non-militant wing of the movement, which made the case for women to be employed in the higher grades of civil service roles. It noted a report from the Royal Commission on the Civil Service had recommended that 'specially qualified women' should be appointed to departments such as the Board of Education, the Local Government Board and the Home Department and be eligible to be appointed for positions in museums and libraries. The letter called for an inquiry to be held to discuss which roles in government departments could be filled by women. The NUWSS memo went on:

> The strain on all the administrative departments is greatly increased by the war. Many of the ablest of the younger officials are at the front. The universities are largely depleted of their men students, and, in consequence, the supply of suitable male candidates for administrative work is, for the time, diminished. But women students, both in degree courses and in post-graduate research fully maintain their numbers; many well-qualified women are acquiring, in various forms of social work, experience which would be of great value in departmental administration; and all of them, like the rest of the nation, are ready to answer the call for devoted public service through which we are passing…It is in all countries where women remain without the franchise difficult for men to realise that the best mode of making use of their services is to give them the highest work they are competent for, and not the lowest.[4]

At the time a register was being compiled to show the qualifications and capacity for service of women who had studied at university, but the memo expresses outrage that the only official recognition of the existence of the degree-educated women and the possible contribution they could make came in the form of a circular to individuals which asked if they could milk cows, or were 'able to engage in other menial agricultural operations':

> It would probably occasion considerable astonishment were a similar inquiry to be officially addressed to the male dons and tutors at Cambridge who are incapacitated by age or otherwise for military service. The principle that 'the stone which is fit for the wall should never be left in the roadway' is even now not understood to be applicable to women. Yet the true interests of every nation consist, surely, in employing its willing and competent citizens in those posts of vantage in which they can most effectively render service.[5]

Between July 1914 and November 1918, the number of working women in the UK rose from 24 per cent to 37 per cent. Around 2 million women replaced men in jobs.[6] The tasks women took on were in many cases unlike work they had undertaken before, from lamplighters to meat sales. Cards issued by Black Cat Cigarettes at the time, which are held in Glasgow Women's Library suffrage collection, illustrate the variation of the jobs, and the novelty of women taking on roles in professions previously dominated by men.

One cigarette card on the subject of the dentist says:

Even in war-time teeth will ache, and as the Dentists can't get men to do the necessary mechanical work, they have had to employ women. A short course of training enables the latter to undertake a good deal of very useful work, and they will probably be required to continue even after the war.

Another depicting a woman in a newspaper office reads:

Before the war, there were a few printing offices which employed women compositors, but not a great many. Now there is a huge number of women employed in newspaper and other printing offices and they are doing splendid work in making it possible for us to get news every day.

In Glasgow, James Dalrymple, the manager of the city's trams, recruited so many of his staff for the war effort that few men were left to run the system. Glasgow became the first city in Britain to recruit women drivers and conductresses during the war, with the novelty of the situation making headlines, such as this report in the *Yorkshire Evening Post* in March 1915:

The Glasgow Tramway Department has begun an experiment in the way of employing women conductors on the cars. Two employees who have had considerable experience of the office work of the departments have been selected with the view of testing the practicability of the scheme, and yesterday made their appearance on two of the routes, and remained on duty throughout the period.

The routes were chosen as being particularly suitable for the employment of the ladies, who have been supplied with a blue uniform, composed of coat, skirt and a cap, with facings. The cap is shaped like that worn by yachtsmen, and gives the wearers a distinctive appearance. The women discharged the duties yesterday remarkably well, although, as a precautionary measure, an inspector travelled on each of the cars with them.[7]

The approach was a cautious one, the two women were initially employed for just a week to see if the trial would be successful. By November of that year, it was reported that another experiment – allowing women to drive trams under the direction of male employees – had also proved a success, so that six women were driving cars 'without any assistance'.[8] In the end, over the course of the war, a total of 1,080 female conductresses and 25 female tram drivers were employed by the city. Among them was Eliza Orr, from the Gorbals, who was married with two children when she started working on the trams as a conductress in 1915. She became a tram driver the following year.[9]

The National Union of Women's Suffrage Societies had a direct link with the war effort, by driving fundraising to set up the Scottish Women's Hospitals for Home and Foreign Service in 1914. Before the war, opportunities for female medics were limited, indeed, it had only been two decades since the first women graduated in medicine from Glasgow University. When war broke out, they were unable to enlist in the Royal Army Medical Corps.[10]

The Scottish Women's Hospitals (SWH) were voluntary and staffed almost entirely by women. They provided doctors and nurses, ambulance drivers and cooks for medical units. By the end of the war a total of fourteen units in the field were in operation in countries including France, Russia, Romania and particularly Serbia. The conditions which the units faced were brutal, as this description of the work at Valjevo in Serbia outlines: 'The Austrians in their retreat left 2,500 dying men there, and of the twelve Serbian doctors who went to their relief six have died. It is in this famine and disease stricken district that our Serbian unit will take up its work.'[11]

The appalling conditions also took a terrible toll on the staff of the SWH, with regular reports of deaths and illness alongside updates on successful fundraising efforts:

> The Scottish hospitals of the National Union are going on with their excellent work, and the handsome sum of £14, 431 has been raised. Sorrow has overtaken the Serbian unit in the loss of two of the staff. Sister Jordan, who nursed Dr Wakefield in typhus, has herself succumbed to it; and Miss Margaret Neil Fraser, a dresser and orderly, well known as a lady golfer, has died from the same terrible plague. A former National Union organiser, Miss Thurstan, who has been more than half over Europe in the 'flying column', has at last been invalided home with a wound and pleurisy. She is enthusiastic about her work, as indeed they all are.[12]

Another report praised SWH member Miss Mary Davies for her courage after 'inoculating herself with the bacillus of gas gangrene in order to test the efficacy of a new method of treatment of gas gangrene in wounds, which has led to so many deaths in this war, and has so far baffled the efforts of surgeons'.[13]

The units were staffed by women from all over the world, who were not necessarily suffragists. The name most associated with the Scottish Women's Hospital is founder Dr Elsie Inglis, who is linked to Edinburgh, where she set up a medical practice. Women from Glasgow who were part of the efforts include Dr Louise McIlroy, who graduated from Glasgow University in 1898 and became the first woman professor of obstetrics and gynaecology of the University of London. She served with the SWH in France as a surgeon, before later going to Serbia and Salonika and lastly becoming a surgeon in Constantinople. She was awarded the Croix de Guerre for her service in 1916 and made an OBE in 1920. She died in 1968 at the age of 90 and one tribute to her published in an obituary in the *British Medical Journal* noted: 'She could not bear the thought that her opinion would be passed unopposed just because she was a woman.'[14]

In just one of the extraordinary incidents in the history of the SWH, nurses had to go on a 300-mile escape over nine weeks to flee from Serbia when the country was overrun by German and Bulgarian forces. The party of twenty-eight female doctors, nurses and orderlies arrived in London 'wearing the clothes in which they had made their flight' and carrying the remnants of their possessions. It was reported that they had to survive on just half-a-pound of bread a day in the worst of the situation:

> The party had encountered a journey of great hardship, and they travelled mostly on foot. They had to climb the Albanian mountains, several thousand feet in height in a blinding snow-storm. Wherever they halted, the party at once started dressing the wounds of the Serbian soldiers, who were being conveyed to the south in bullock wagons, which was the only mode of transport for the Serbian wounded. The nurses took part in the Serbian retreat, which, although conducted in a masterly manner was in great confusion owing to the impassable condition of the roads and in many cases owing to there being no roads at all.
>
> The Scottish party travelled overland through Italy and France, and they met with the greatest courtesy and kindness from the military authorities in these countries.[15]

The Territorial Force Nursing Service, which was established in 1908, also saw many women take part in the war effort. Among them were the Carruthers sisters, Kate – or Catherine – and Margaret from Glasgow, who were sent to France in 1915. Kate was awarded the Military Medal for bravery in the field.

Another nurse who served overseas with the Territorial Force Nursing Service was Agnes Climie, from Cathcart, who was sent to a field hospital at St Omer in France. She was killed at the age of 32 after the hospital was hit by a prolonged air raid.[16]

At home, women were drafted in to help in the war industry, such as manufacturing of munitions. A report in November 1915 noted:

The employment of women in work rendered necessary by the withdrawal of men for service in the Army continues to increase. Women are now admitted to more Government munition factories and to certain departments of munition work and aeroplane making hitherto confined to men. The Government has announced that women employed in these factories on time-work usually done by men shall receive £1 a week. The same overtime, night-shift, Sunday and holiday allowances payable to men will be paid to women. For piece-work women will also receive the same wages as men, and where payment is made by results equal payment will be made to women as to men for equal amount of work done.[17]

A report in 1915 noted that while much had been written about women undertaking work on tramways, railways, factories and shops, there was little known about the female workers undertaking the 'arduous work' in munitions factories:

They do not appear so much in the public eye, as do the lady conductors, porters and ticket collectors, but their work has an immediate and direct influence upon the fortunes of the war, and their patriotic efforts have been successful beyond the expectations of those who were most sanguine regarding the experiment, and have more than astonished their employers and male workmates.[18]

The women were reported to be able to undertake practically every stage of the work, which included manufacturing 18lb high-explosive shells, and only some tasks which 'might prove beyond the strength of women' were undertaken by men:

The women take the rough piece of bar steel, weighing about twenty-eight pounds, which forms the raw material, pass it through the various lathes, turning, drilling and boring it, and perform the various operations in a manner which produces articles exactly to gauge and earns the admiration of their overseers. Indeed so keen are they, and so skilled have they become, that they have succeeded in turning out more work than some of the machines were believed to be capable of producing.[19]

In Glasgow, three factories were built at Mossend, Mile End and Cardonald to manufacture artillery guns and shells. Lizzie Robinson worked in Cardonald and was awarded the Medal of the Order of the British Empire for her devotion to her duties, working seven days a week over eighteen months without missing a shift.[20]

> Another recipient of a war honour who received a special ovation from the crowd was a woman munition worker, Miss Lizzie Robinson, upon whom the king conferred the medal of the British Empire Order. She is employed in the National Projectile Factory at Cardonald. The wounded soldiers gave Miss Robinson as she was passing them a special round of applause.[21]

However, such work wasn't entirely without any problems, as a strike by 400 women employed by Messrs Beardmore at its factory in East Hope Street in 1917 showed. The issue was raised in the House of Commons where it was stated that the origin of the strike was the dismissal of four women who were accused of restricting output:

> Three of the women have been in the employment of the firm for two years…they catch a 5.25 train every morning, and do not return home until 7.25 at night…one of them was the most successful fine borer engaged by the firm in 1916, and gained the highest bonus for ten weeks in succession, and that she now attributes her decreased output to the state of her health, due to the strain of the long hours… the fourth woman is the mother of four children, and, in addition to her work, has had to look after them and attend to a paralysed husband, who died three weeks ago.[22]

In addition to taking up roles in the working world, other women concentrated their efforts on organising supplies and provisions for the men fighting abroad. In Glasgow, Isabella Lilburn set up a donations depot at a hotel in Charing Cross to gather everyday items to be sent to soldiers on the frontline, such as soap and hand-knitted socks. [23]

The role of women changed as a result of the war, and with it came recognition that they could undertake work previously thought to only be the domain of men. An acknowledgement of this was made in the journal *Engineer*:

In fact, it can be stated with absolute truth that with the possible exception of the heaviest tools – and their inability to work even these has yet to be established – women have shown themselves perfectly capable of performing operations which hitherto have been exclusively carried out by men.[24]

An editorial in the *Glasgow Herald* also outlined the stark shift in attitudes. It cited an appeal for reserve forces of woman workers throughout the country – whether trained or not – to be registered and then mobilised as 'proof of the utter collapse under the stress of war of sex-exclusiveness and prejudice against women workers':

Women have been 'in business' for so many years that one need merely refer to the fact that there are still thousands of men of military age in every large city who could be released from clerical work by women. The girl who has just left business training classes could not step at once into the place vacated by an insurance clerk who, at the age of 33, let us say, has had four or five years' experience. But she would be ready to take the place of a junior clerk promoted. That is merely one example of many kinds of clerical work from which it will be necessary to release men whose proper place is present in with the colours. There is scope for women as railway-ticket and parcel clerks, in many shop departments at present staffed by men, and even in the production of certain kinds of war material.

It acknowledged that women taking up different roles in society would have a longer-term impact in the future. 'No doubt the influx of women into many new employments may raise some more or less anxious problems after the War is over. But we need not try to cross any of these bridges until we come to them.'[25]

From the horrors of war emerged a hope that women, in demonstrating their capacity to play a far more active role outside the home, would be allowed to play a fuller part in society. In 1916, the *Votes for Women* newspaper carried a list of 'Some reasons why adult suffrage is now within the sphere of practical politics' which included points such as:

> Because by no other measure can the will of the whole people be expressed in the Parliament which will have to deal with reconstruction after the War…Because even the Prime Minister, the strongest opponent in pre-war days of Woman Suffrage, now admits that the claim of women to be included in such a Bill has become 'unanswerable'… Because no measure short of manhood suffrage will secure the votes of fighting men and male war workers; and no measure short of womanhood suffrage will secure votes equally to the women doing war work and in a multitude of ways keeping the country going at home.[26]

Prominent suffragist Millicent Garrett Fawcett, who became the leader of the National Union of Women's Suffrage Societies, summed it up in a famous quote when she said:

> The war revolutionised the industrial position of women. It found them serfs and left them free. It not only opened opportunities of employment in a number of skilled trades, but, more important even than this, it revolutionised men's minds and their conception of the sort of work of which the ordinary everyday woman was capable.[27]

However, it wasn't only in the context of war that women had been forging ahead. In the late nineteenth and early twentieth centuries there are examples of astute businesswomen in Glasgow who have left a lasting legacy in the city. Miss Catherine Cranston – also known as Kate – was a pioneer of tearooms and opened four establishments, the first of which was in Argyle Street in 1878. She was also a leader when it came to patronage of the arts, using artists Charles Rennie Mackintosh and his wife Margaret Macdonald to design the Willow Tea Rooms in Sauchiehall Street. The opening of her venture at 91 Buchanan Street in Glasgow in 1897 was described in the glowing terms as 'one of the most complete and finest-equipped dining establishments in the Kingdom'.

> The name of Cranston has long been associated with this particular line of business, and the honourable reputation of the past is sufficient guarantee of what may be expected from the latest addition to Glasgow's restaurants....Before entering on this, her latest venture, Miss Cranston made a study of the home and Continental dining establishments, and the result of her careful investigations and inquiries is now seen in her new rooms, which, in the opinion of those well qualified to judge, eclipse anything of the kind yet attempted in this country.[28]

And the description indeed indicates it was a lavish venture:

> There are in all four flats, with two rooms in each. A beautiful staircase connects all the storeys, and communication between them is also obtained by means of an elevator. The front room on the ground floor – the ladies' tea-room – is furnished with solid oak in imitation of an old English inn, while the room behind, which is set aside as the gentleman's tea-room, is also artistically furnished. The two rooms on the second flat – the ladies' and gentlemen's dining-rooms – are prettily decorated with floral emblems, and the two rooms on the floor above also present a handsome appearance, the front one being treated in a Dutch fashion. The billiard and smoking-rooms are located on the top storey, and the decorations of these are in full harmony with the other portions of the building.[29]

Miss Cranston's tea-rooms were part of a popular and fashionable movement, particularly appealing to wealthier women. But when her husband John Cochrane died in 1917 she sold most of her businesses and withdrew from public life. When she died in 1934 at the age of 85, she left her estate to charity, with directions that the majority – two-thirds – be used to benefit the poor in Glasgow.[30]

For nearly 40 years she was associated with the catering industry in Glasgow and it was her flair for the novel and unexpected which led to the banishing of stereotyped furnishings in the city tearooms... Miss Cranston early saw the possibilities in tearooms and restaurants. Gifted with original ideas and keen business capacity, she decided to strike along a new line, and in doing so immediately encountered success...Her establishments were deemed perfect in cuisine and artistic effect, and everything in them was distinctive.[31]

Indeed one of the establishments which she founded is still in existence today. The Willow Tearooms, in Sauchiehall Street, which first opened for business in 1903 and was designed by Charles Rennie Mackintosh, recently underwent a two-year refurbishment and reopened at the time of writing.

Another pioneering Glasgow businesswoman was Maggie McIver, who founded The Barras market and the Barrowland Ballroom, two of the most famous institutions of the city. She was born in Galston, in Ayrshire and as a child came to Glasgow with her parents.[32] Along with her husband James, she organised a Saturday market which grew to attract hundreds of stallholders. When James died, her enterprising activities continued with the opening of the Barrowland Ballroom on Christmas Eve in 1934, a venture to take advantage of the growing popularity of dance halls in the city. It, of course, remains world famous today as a music venue. When she died in May 1958, Maggie, the daughter of a French polisher and a policeman, was a multi-millionaire and had become known as the 'Queen of the Barras'.

In 1939, plans to add a £50,000 ice rink and an entirely new market at the Barrowland made the front page of the *Daily Record* newspaper. The new venture was also to include a heavily reinforced roof with 18 inches of concrete in case it could be used as an air-raid shelter in the future. It was noted that 400 people in Glasgow and England were reliant on the market for work, and the reports also included a summary of the history of "The woman they call 'The Boss'" – Margaret MacIver or M'Iver, as surnames were commonly written then. It notes that she left her job as a

French polisher when she was 19 to pursue a healthier outdoor life and started selling fruit, hiring a barrow by the day, with the business soon growing from shillings to pounds, to hundreds then thousands of pounds:

> Margaret Russell's single-barrow career lasted only a few years. A pony and float costing £6 was the next acquisition. Business was on the upgrade, and, when Margaret married M'Iver, who was in the fruit trade, it simply rushed ahead. Three or four shops were started in the East End. The M'Ivers weren't only retail. With floats and shops, they were also large-scale distributors to other dealers.[33]

When Margaret purchased ground at Kent Street, 'The Barrows' was set up and soon there was a flourishing market, followed by the Barrowland Palais – the ballroom – which is 'so popular that extension is essential'. Margaret, who had a family of fourteen children as well as setting up her business empire – of whom just six were still alive in 1939 – described her typical day: 'It has been a great life. Up at four in the morning, in bed after midnight. Hard work doesn't kill anybody. Even when I wisnae hard at it, I always kept an eye on the business. I couldnae help myself.'[34]

CHAPTER SEVEN

Radical Women and the First Politicians: 'Fulfilling Hopes'

As the war progressed, so the recognition of the vital role women were playing in society grew. The Representation of the People Bill, which was to eventually enfranchise women over the age of 21, had passed its second reading by May 1917. The Glasgow Society for Women's Suffrage was for the first time able to report that the long efforts to secure the vote for women were at last paying off:

> Events momentous in the history of Women's Suffrage fall to be reported this year. Twelve months ago the situation was not hopeful. The realization [*sic*] of the aims for which all Suffragists were working appeared to be no nearer than before. Now the position is entirely altered. Not only is opinion in the country almost unanimously in favour of the enfranchisement of women, but the principle has been accepted by the House of Commons and has been embodied in a Government Bill. The end is not yet won, but surely it may be said that the goal is in sight…
> It is estimated that the number of women to be enfranchised by the Bill will be about 6,000,000, of whom 5,000,000 will be married women.[1]

Of course not all were yet in favour. Speaking in a House of Lords debate in January 1918, Lord George Curzon, the President of the National League for Opposing Woman Suffrage, outlined his opposition to the move, despite acknowledging 'powerful speeches' in favour of it:

I personally remain unconvinced that it is either fair, or desirable, or wise, in the manner that is proposed, to add 6,000,000 female voters to the electorate of this country...In the first place, as many speakers have pointed out, this is a vast and incalculable, almost a catastrophic, change which, whatever may be your views about it, is without precedent in history and without justification in experience. I own, my Lords, that personally I am not very much impressed by the example of Finland and Norway and the fourteen States of America, nor even of California, upon which stress was laid by the noble Earl, Lord Russell, a few minutes ago, nor even of New Zealand or Saskatchewan. The action and examples of those communities, important as they are, all leave me in this connection absolutely cold and unmoved. No one can dispute the fact that no great State in history has ever made, so far, such a change... while the example of Russia, which I believe has conceded at one swoop universal suffrage, male and female, does not fill me with any positive enthusiasm.[2]

The Glasgow Society for Women's Suffrage did note that the enfranchisement of women proposed in the Bill fell far short of what they were seeking – which was to obtain the vote on the same terms as men – but acknowledged it as a first step with the principle that women should be able to go to the ballot box at last being conceded. When the act became law, it was given a cautious welcome by the society:

The Representation of the People Bill passed into law on the 6th day of February 1918, thus marking an epoch in the Women's Suffrage movement, by granting to women for the first time the right to be registered as parliamentary voters. While welcoming whole-heartedly this measure of justice, your Committee does not forget that this right has been granted to a limited number of women and on very irrational grounds. It therefore leaves much work to be done by Suffrage Societies in order to gain real equality as between men and women.[3]

By the 1920s, the society had evolved in the Glasgow Society for Equal Citizenship, which had the aim of obtaining the 'parliamentary franchise for women on the same terms as it is or may be granted to men'. It also campaigned on other issues, for example, in the annual report of 1921–22 it was noted that action on the Criminal Law Amendment Bill had been successful:

> This may be regarded as a triumph for Women's Societies, because it was as the result of great pressure from the Women's Organisations that the Government introduced its Bill on this subject. It did not go through without difficulty owing to the opposition of a persistent group of opponents. The most important Clauses are those which:-
>
> (a) Raise the age for indecent assault from 13 to 16.
> (b) Take away the plea of reasonable cause to believe that a girl is under the age of 16, except in the case of young men of 23 and under, on the occasion of a first offence.
> (c) Extend the time limit during which proceedings can be taken in a case of criminal assault, from six to nine months after the offence.[4]

There were other social issues in which women in Glasgow were playing a prominent role, most notably, the rent strikes of 1915, in which women fought against landlords taking advantage of the wartime economy. A boom in shipyard and munitions workers had led to the hiking up of rents as the population grew and accommodation became scarce. One of the key figures in the campaign against the increasing rents in Govan was Mary Barbour, who was born in 1875 in Kilbarchan, Renfrewshire. She became involved in tenants' committees and organised resistance against eviction action by landlords, as thousands of people fell into rent arrears in the city.

One such demonstration involved 800 women and children marching to the City Chambers in October 1915. Many of the women affected by the proposed increase of rents were the wives of soldiers fighting at the front, which they fully utilised to draw widespread support to their cause:

They carried banners bearing mottos such as 'Our husbands, sons and brothers are fighting the Prussians of Germany. We are fighting the Prussians of Partick. Only alternative – Municipal housing'. 'Government must protect our homes from Germans and landlords or the people will protect themselves.'

A party of little Dennistoun boys and girls carried banners bearing the words 'While my father is a prisoner in Germany the landlord is attacking our home': 'My father is fighting in France. We are fighting the Huns at home.'[5]

A deputation – composed almost entirely of women and representing twenty districts of the city – was subsequently admitted to the Council Chamber. Members of the council were told that one of the principal causes of increasing rents was the 'gradual and now entire cessation of house-building and the monopoly being in the hands of private owners' and that the 'citizens were now within measurable distance of a house famine'.

The matter prompted some angry exchanges among councillors, when it was voted to delay discussing the issue until the next meeting:

Mr Izett hotly declared that 'all these people will be evicted if you don't take up this question today.' The Chairman, rapping the desk with the gavel, announced that the matter was at an end for that day.

Mr Izett – 'It does not matter a d_____ for you: we are not going to have the women and children put out on the street, I hold that this Council is responsible.'

The Chairman – 'You must withdraw that expression.'

Mr Izett – 'I will not: certainly not. You cowardly lot that you are.'[6]

The first attempts at evicting tenants who were participating in rent strikes took place towards the end of October 1915, according to reports – but the protesters were determined not to let the first one go ahead. A widow, who was said to be ill, living in Merryland Street in Govan was due to be turfed out of her accommodation, but the action was met with resistance including the use of household ingredients such as flour:

While Mrs Barbour, of the Glasgow Women's Housing Association, was addressing those who had assembled, two sheriff officers arrived and endeavoured to gain admission to the house. As soon as it was known that it was proposed to eject the tenant the demonstrators determined to resist. Most of them were women, and they attacked the officers and their assistants with peasemeal, flour and whiting. A woman was arrested on a charge of assaulting one of the officers. She was taken to the Govan Police Office, but was not detained.[7]

The incident concluded after a consultation between Mrs Barbour and the officer, the report notes. The officer was able to enter the house afterwards, but when it was pointed out that the tenant was ill the officer 'decided not to proceed with the enforcement of the warrant'. A decided victory for Mrs Barbour's army.

By November 1915, the rent strikes were spreading beyond Glasgow to other areas of the country and as many as 20,000 tenants were on rent strike.[8] It reached crisis point when Partick factor Daniel Nicholson sought the prosecution of eighteen strikers, including fifteen munitions workers. On 17 November there were 'lively scenes' when 'several thousand people' took to the streets to show their disgust at the move.[9]

A test case was taken against a householder called Mr Reid, who was the secretary of the Tenants' Defence Committee, and had refused to pay an increased rent of £2 1s 2d per month. He told the court that the old rent he had been paying was £1 19s and 2d – 2s less per month – and that pre-war the rent was just £1 18s. The cases were dropped following an intervention by a government minister. The sheriff wisely decided to take into account a letter sent directly from the Minister of Munitions to the factor Mr Nicholson, which asked for the cases either to be dropped or continued with a view to new legislation on the issue, which was promised would soon come into force.

While this court session was going on, demonstrators had taken to the streets once again to show their disgust at the rent increases:

Two processions proceed to the County buildings through the central parts of the city, their appearance everywhere arousing a good deal of public interest. The main body was preceded by a band with improvised instruments, including tin whistles, 'hooters', and a dilapidated big drum. A number of the men carried pieces of lighted candle and some of them bore wooden signs announcing houses and shops to let. The crowd passed through George Square and in front of the City Chambers. Except for a good deal of shouting and cheering, and the sounding of the whistles and 'hooters' no demonstration took place in the Square. The police had been warned of the approach of the demonstrators and when the latter arrived at the County Buildings they found the entrance barred by constables. The crowd marched round the building cheering good humouredly and came to a standstill... facing the entrance to the Small Debt Court.[10]

When the result of the proceedings in court became known, it was greeted with 'much cheering'. The Rent Restrictions Act, which placed limits on increases in rent and the rate of mortgage interest during the First World War to prevent landlords profiteering from the shortage of housing, was in place by 25 November 1915. More than 100 years later, Mary Barbour's role in the remarkable campaign was commemorated with a statue in Govan, which was unveiled in March 2018.

Another woman involved in the rent strike was Jane Rae, one of the leaders of an all-out-strike in the Singer sewing machine factory, which employed 3,000 women. She was born in Bonnybridge in 1872 and later moved to Clydebank with her family. The Singer strike began in March 1911, when anger at changes to working conditions at the factory – resulting in more work for less pay for many – boiled over into industrial action. Twelve cabinet polishers were the first to walk out and within two days they were joined by nearly all their 11,000 colleagues. It was reported with little sympathy by the *Dundee Evening Telegraph* under the headline: 'Half-A-Dozen Girls are asked to do certain work and there is a strike at Singer's Factory by which 11,000 are thrown idle':

Wiring late this afternoon, our Glasgow correspondent says- 'The conference in regard to the strike has proved abortive, and nearly 11,000 employees are now idle. A mass meeting has been arranged for Thursday. Lively scenes have occurred today in the vicinity of the works. Large squads of men and women left at the dinner hour and augmented the ranks of the strikers, who paraded the streets headed by a brass band.'

It went on: 'It is alleged the present dispute over the wages question has been fermenting for some time, but was brought to a head today owing to half a dozen girls, who were piece-workers, being asked to do work previously done by time-workers.'[11]

Attempts by the workers to meet with management were refused and in the end a ballot was held to determine whether they would return to work. As Jane Rae pointed out, it was the first time women had been able to vote – but the result was the majority voting in favour of ending the strike, with an unconditional return to work on 10 April 1911. Subsequently more than 400 of the workers who had been key leaders and activists in the dispute were sacked – including Jane. Undeterred, she continued to fight for workers' rights and became one of the first female councillors in Scotland in 1922, when she was elected for the Labour party for Clydebank Town Council. A plaque to commemorate her life is now in the gardens of Clydebank Town Hall.

In 1918, as well as some women gaining the right to vote, women were also allowed to become MPs for the first time. This was enabled under a short act called the Parliament (Qualification of Women) Act, which was just one page long and stated: 'A woman shall not be disqualified by sex or marriage for being elected to or sitting or voting as a Member of the Commons House of Parliament.'

Unlike the right to vote – which applied to women over the age of 30 who met certain property qualification – there were no age restrictions on women being MPs. So they could be elected from the age of 21, the same as men. *The Vote*, the newspaper of the Women's Freedom League, published a list of the candidates and an impassioned plea on the front page ahead of the election:

The General Election will be historic in our annals. For the first time in this country women will have the right both to vote for their representatives in the House of Commons and to stand as candidates. The effect on male politicians is to make women 'more of a mystery than ever'; the effect on women is to bring home to them their responsibility in choosing the best candidate to represent them in a Parliament which will have to undertake no less a task than the reconstruction of national life. In such responsible work the best brains and heart of the nation must unite; women must be returned to the new Parliament. Let men and women electors, putting aside prejudice and inexperience, see that women are able to take their places side by side with men in legislating for the national welfare.[12]

In the election of December 1918, seventeen women stood for election, with just one in Scotland, Eunice Murray, who was a leading figure in the Women's Franchise League. She stood as an independent candidate for Bridgeton, Glasgow. In a short address at a ceremony planting a tree at Falkirk Municipal Buildings to commemorate the enfranchisement of women she spoke of the change in attitudes towards women:

Before the war they were sometimes called 'sexless females', but today they heard a paean of praise for women and they lived in such a 'purring' atmosphere and heard such expressions as 'Women are simply splendid' or 'Women are simply wonderful' that it might be thought women had become very different to what they were before the war. She did not hold with that, because she knew women were just the same as they were before the war but they had obtained their opportunity. (Applause). The vote had been given to women during the greatest crisis in the history of their country, and if men were unreasonable – and some were – (laughter) – in withholding the vote, they were generous when they gave it. They gave it at a moment when few other nations would have the courage to give the vote to six million women.[13]

She went on to highlight the role which she hoped women would play after entering the political world:

In the future they would have many great questions to tackle, and they had to remember that legislation entered every home in the State, the State itself being only a big home. She thought every man would agree with her that men by themselves had made a great muddle of things. (Laughter). She thought every man would agree that Europe was in a sad way because they did not ask the help of women before, and she believed the first gift women would bring to the counsels of the nation would be a new idealism. She believed when the great days of reconstruction came, when peace had dawned, that the peace would be more lasting and would be a better peace because women as well as men had a say in it.[14]

In the end, Eunice did not get elected and was one of at least seven candidates for Glasgow who had to forfeit the £150 deposit paid to stand for election, after failing to secure one-eighth of the total vote in the constituencies for which they stood. The only woman to win a seat in 1918 was Irish politician Countess Constance Markievicz, who had taken part in the Easter Rising in 1916. However, she did not take up her seat in Westminster for the constituency of Dublin St Patrick's, in line with the policy of her party, Sinn Fein.

It was to be another five years before a woman in Scotland became an MP, with the election of aristocrat Katharine Stewart Murray, the Duchess of Atholl, who won her seat in Perth and Kinross for the Conservatives in the general election of 6 December 1923. In March 1929, Janet – or 'Jennie' – Lee was elected as Labour MP for North Lanarkshire. At the age of 24, she was able to take up a seat at Westminster but was too young to vote, as the Equal Franchise Act was yet to come into force. It was in place for the general election in May that year.

However, it wasn't until September 1937 when a constituency in Glasgow was represented by a woman. Agnes Hardie won the Glasgow Springburn seat for Labour in a by-election triggered by the death of her predecessor – and husband – George Hardie, the younger brother of the party's founder Keir Hardie. Her first contribution in Parliament was to a debate on the introduction of a bill which aimed to give workers paid holidays, in which she highlighted the circumstances of women in her home city in particular:

I come from Glasgow and I can assure hon. Members that those who live in the Glasgow working-class areas need holidays very badly. We know that, from one year to another, many of these people skimp, and save in order to be able to get a fortnight at the coast. This consideration particularly concerns the women and children. The woman who has to live in a room and kitchen or even in a two-room and kitchen house, if she is aristocratic enough to be able to afford one—and that is about the upper limit in housing for the working-classes in Scotland—has a very hard life in very sordid surroundings. This has a tremendous effect on the health of the people in the big cities.

She went on:

Some years ago the Glasgow council as a result of an agitation by the Labour members, decided to take some Glasgow mothers for a sail down the Clyde. It was discovered that there were mothers and grandmothers who had never been out of Glasgow all their lives and had never even had a sail down the Clyde, because they had not been able to afford it. We are asking the House to see that the husbands of women such as these should get holidays with pay, and so be able to take their wives and children for a much needed change every year.[15]

Nearly twenty years after women first won the right to vote, the voice of a woman representing Glasgow was finally being heard in Parliament. The long road to participating in political life had begun back in 1867 when the first Suffrage Bill was introduced in Parliament, through to the Equal Franchise Act in 1928, which ensured women could vote on the same terms as men in the general election in May the following year. It also had the effect of adding more than 5 million women to the voters' roll, and indeed making them the majority of the electorate at 52.7 per cent.[16]

The Glasgow Society for Equal Citizenship noted the progress that had been made following this change, recording that it is with 'profound satisfaction' that the 'great reform worked for during so many years has now been obtained':

John Stuart Mill, when he introduced the first Women's Suffrage Bill in 1867, ventured upon a prophecy. 'When the time comes, as it certainly will come,' he said, 'when this reform will be granted, I feel the firmest conviction that you will never repent of the concession.'

Mr Baldwin, when he introduced the last Women's Suffrage Bill in 1928, went even further. 'It may well be,' he said, 'that men and women, working together for the regeneration of their country, and for the regeneration of the world, each doing that for which they are better fitted, may provide such an environment that each immortal soul as it is born on this earth may have a fairer chance and a fairer home than has ever yet been vouchsafed to the generations that have passed. It is for the future to fulfil these hopes.'

And so what has the future looked like? Today, at the time of writing, there is a woman at the very top of Westminster, Prime Minister Theresa May of the Conservatives. But she is only the second female prime minister in Britain, after Margaret Thatcher and the first of the twenty-first century. In the General Election of 2017, a record 208 women MPs were elected to the House of Commons, but they still only make up 32 per cent of the total. In the House of Lords there are 206 female peers, accounting for just 26 per cent of the total.[17]

In the Scottish Parliament, the First Minister is Nicola Sturgeon, who represents the Glasgow constituency of Govan. The leader of the Conservative opposition is also a woman, Ruth Davidson. But following the most recent election in 2016, a total of forty-five women were elected, the same as in the election five years previously, compared to eighty-four men, making up just 35 per cent of the total. In many other areas of public life, women in Scotland – who make up 52 per cent of the population – are also vastly underrepresented, for example making up just 25 per cent of local councillors and only 25 per cent of company directors.[18] There can be no denying that huge progress has been made, but the debate over inequality and lack of gender balance at the top levels of society, and how to make sure that women are more represented in areas such as the public sector and political sphere, still rages on.

On 10 June 2018, women from across the UK marched together to mark the 100 year anniversary of women winning the right to vote. Events took place in London, Belfast, Cardiff and Edinburgh, and just like the original movement, included many women from Glasgow who travelled to take part in the occasion. The participants were given scarves to wear in one of the suffragette colours, green, white or purple, to create the effect of a vast flag unfurling across the cities and the marches finished underneath an arch with the message 'My Vote *Really* Makes a Difference'.

In the past century since women won the vote, much has changed in the world and society. But what's also striking is that some of the issues that were raised by the early pioneering women of Glasgow are still relevant today – the concern over equal pay and the right to a living wage is far from unfamiliar to modern debates. While women are now playing their part in political life, the existence of campaigns to gain at least 50 per cent representation of women in Parliament shows there is a long way to go.

The oak tree that was planted in celebration by the suffragettes in Glasgow stands just a few yards from the pavement in Kelvin Way, in among the numerous trees that line the elegant street. It's easy to walk by without noticing, just like it's easy to miss the stories of the women of Glasgow who fought for equality on so many fronts. They should not be forgotten.

Acknowledgements

With grateful thanks to the staff at the following for their help and assistance during the research for this book:

The Mitchell Library, Glasgow
Glasgow Women's Library
The British Newspaper Archive
Scottish Poetry Library
Glasgow University Archive Services
Strathclyde University Andersonian Library

Select Bibliography

Cohen, Edward H., Fertig, Anne R., and Fleming, Linda, *A Song of Glasgow Town: The Collected Poems of Marion Bernstein* (The Association for Scottish Literary Studies, 2013)

Craig, Maggie, *When the Clyde Ran Red* (Mainstream Publishing, 2011)

Faley, Jean, *Up Oor Close: Memories of Domestic Life in Glasgow Tenements, 1910 -1945* (White Cockade Publishing, 1990)

Hawksley, Lucinda, *March Women March: How Women Won the Vote* (Andre Deutsch, 2013)

King, Elspeth, *The Hidden History of Glasgow's Women* (Mainstream Publishing, 1993)

Lynch, Michael, *Oxford Companion to Scottish History* (Oxford University Press, 2011)

Pankhurst, Sylvia E., *The Suffragette Movement: An Intimate Account of Persons and Ideals* (Wharton Press, 2013)

Swift, Helen Susan, *Women of Scotland: A Journey to Scottish History* (Creativia, 2013)

Notes

Introduction: 'The Door Is Open'

1. www.parliament.uk/about/living-heritage/transformingsociety/
   electionsvoting/womenvote/overview/thevote/
2. The *Sunday Post* Special, 21 April 1918.
3. The *Glasgow Herald*, 14 December 1918.
4. *The Scotsman*, 16 December 1918.
5. *The Scotsman*, 16 December 1918.
6. *The Scotsman*, 16 December 1918.
7. *Sunday Post*, 15 December 1918.
8. The *Glasgow Herald*, 16 December 1918.
9. *The Scotsman*, 16 December 1918.
10. The *Glasgow Herald*, 16 December 1918.
11. *Daily Record*, 17 December 1918.
12. *Britannia*, 11 January 1918.
13. The *Glasgow Herald*, 22 April 1918.

Chapter One: Education: 'Keep knocking at the gates'

1. xiv Scottish Funding Council, Higher Education Students and
   Qualifiers at Scottish Institutions 2016-2017.
2. xv Michael Lynch, *Oxford Companion to Scottish History*.
   Published 2011 by Oxford University Press, p 648.
3. xvi David Murray, *Miss Janet Anne Galloway and the Higher
   Education of Women in Glasgow*. Published 1914, Glasgow,
   James MacLehose and Sons.
4. 'Women Students at Anderson's Institution': ww.strath.ac.uk/
   archives/iotm/june2012/
5. *The Book of the Jubilee: In Commemoration of the Ninth
   Jubilee of the University of Glasgow 1431-1901*. Published
   James MacLehose and Sons, 1901.

6. ibid.
7. ibid.
8. Geyer-Kordesch, G. & Ferguson, R., *Blue stockings, black gowns, white coats*, University of Glasgow, 1994.
9. 'The University of Glasgow Story': www.universitystory.gla.ac.uk/women-background/
10. The *Glasgow Herald*, 12 November 1877.
11. The *Glasgow Herald*, 5 April 1879.
12. The *Glasgow Herald*, 14 November 1882.
13. Ibid.
14. Ibid
15. 'The Glasgow Association for the Higher Education of Women 1878 to 1883', Christine D. Myers, *The Historian*, 9 October 2007.
16. The *Glasgow Herald*, 10 January 1884.
17. Joan McAlpine, *The Lady of Claremont House: Isabella Elder, Pioneer and Philanthropist*. Published 1997, Argyll Publishing.
18. The *Glasgow Herald*, 29 June 1885.
19. ibid.
20. Olive Checkland, *Queen Margaret Union 1890-1980: Women in the University of Glasgow*. Published 1979.
21. *The Book of the Jubilee: In Commemoration of the Ninth Jubilee of the University of Glasgow 1431-1901*. Published by James MacLehose and Sons, 1901.
22. ibid.
23. ibid.
24. ibid.
25. ibid.
26. David Murray, *Miss Janet Anne Galloway and the Higher Education of Women in Glasgow*. Published by James MacLehose and Sons, 1914, Glasgow.
27. 'The University of Glasgow Story': universitystory.gla.ac.uk/biography/?id=WH1111&type=P
28. *The Book of the Jubilee: In Commemoration of the Ninth Jubilee of the University of Glasgow 1431-1901*. Published by James MacLehose and Sons, 1901.

29. ibid.
30. 'The University of Glasgow Story': universitystory.gla.ac.uk/women-background/
31. Olive Checkland, *Queen Margaret Union 1890-1980: Women in the University of Glasgow*. Published 1979.
32. The *Glasgow Herald*, 13 July 1963.
33. BBC News: 'The first female professor in the UK': bbc.co.uk/news/uk-scotland-39191297
34. *The Book of the Jubilee: In Commemoration of the Ninth Jubilee of the University of Glasgow 1431-1901*. Published James MacLehose and Sons, 1901.
35. ibid.

Chapter Two: Work: 'The hopes of tomorrow'

1. The *Dundee Advertiser*, 2 November 1889.
2. 'Patterns of Employment of Working-Class Women in Glasgow 1890-1914', by Alice Jacqueline Mary Albert (Thesis published 1977).
3. Michael Lynch, *Oxford Companion to Scottish History*. Published by Oxford University Press, 2011, p 649.
4. ibid.
5. The *Glasgow Herald*, 1 April 1895.
6. Proceedings of the Philosophical Society of Glasgow 1894-1897, p 70 – 'Women's Industries in Scotland', by Miss Margaret H. Irwin, Assistant Commissioner, late Royal Commission on Labour.
7. Renfrewshire Co-operative Conference Association, 'The Problem of Home Work', by Margaret H. Irwin. With a preface by Professor George Adam Smith DD, LL.D Read at Paisley, on Saturday, 14 December 1901.
8. ibid.
9. The *Glasgow Herald*, 1 April 1895.
10. 'Women Shop Assistants: How They Live and Work: The evidence given by Miss Irwin before the Select Committee of the House of Lords on early closing of shops'. Excerpt from Minute of the Committee 29 April 1901.
11. ibid.

12. Hansard: HC Deb 19 June 1891 Vol 354 cc907-81.
13. 'Women's Work in Tailoring and Dressmaking: Report of an inquiry conducted for the Scottish Council for Women's Trades by Margaret Irwin', published 1900.
14. ibid.
15. The *Glasgow Herald*, 22 January 1940.
16. *Edinburgh Evening News*, 7 August 1900.
17. *Yorkshire Post*, 20 November 1907.
18. Susan Yeandle, *Women of Courage: 100 years of Lady Factory Inspectors*. Published by The Stationery Office, 1993, p 8.
19. 'Who's Who of Glasgow 1909: A Biographical Dictionary of Nearly Five Hundred Living Citizens' (And of Notable Citizens who have died since 1st January 1907).
20. Calton Heritage and Learning Centre: Memorial Garden: caltonhlc.co.uk/about-us/garden/

Chapter Three: Health: 'Smashed human lives'
 1. Understanding Glasgow: The Glasgow Indicators Project: Trends www.understandingglasgow.com/indicators/health/trends/male_life_expectancy_trends_in_scottish_cities.
 2. John K. McDowall, *The People's History of Glasgow*. Published by Hay Nisbet & Co, 1899.
 3. *The Victoria Infirmary of Glasgow, 1890-1990: A Centenary History* Edited by S.D. Slater and D.A. Dow. Published 1990.
 4. 'The Scottish Public Health Observatory: Pregnancy, births and maternity: maternal and birth outcomes': www.scotpho.org.uk/population-dynamics/pregnancy-births-and-maternity/data/maternal-and-birth-outcomes
 5. Hansard: HL Deb 06 July 1903, Vol 124 cc1324-56.
 6. *Daily Record* and *Mail*, July 18, 1918.
 7. The *Evening Telegraph* and *Post*, 22 October 1918.
 8. *Daily Record* and *Mail*, Wednesday, 16 October 1918.
 9. The *Aberdeen Weekly Journal*, 8 January 1902.
10. *Glasgow Royal Maternity: A Brief account of its formation, history and activities*, published circa 1927.
11. *A Visit to the Glasgow Hospital for Sick Children*, published 1883 James MaceLhose and Sons.

12. ibid.
13. ibid.
14. ibid.
15. ibid.
16. *Constitution and Rules of the Glasgow Samaritan Hospital for Women*, published by William Munro, 1891.
17. 'Royal Samaritan Hospital for Women Annual Reports: Glasgow Samaritan Hospital for Women: First Annual Meeting' [Held on Tuesday, 1st February 1887].
18. *Glasgow Evening Times*, 11 February 1888.
19. Glasgow Samaritan Hospital annual report, year ending 31st December 1899.
20. Redlands Hospital for Women Annual Reports 1916-1944.
21. *The Vote*, 20 January 1933.
22. *Glasgow Herald*, 27 February 1932.
23. ibid.
24. *The Scotsman*, 19 April 1913.
25. *Edinburgh Evening News*, 21 December 1905.
26. *Glasgow Herald*, 20 August 1943.
27. ibid.
28. ibid.

Chapter Four: Suffrage: 'I want my vote!'

1. 'Suffrage Fallacies' Sir Almroth Wright on 'Militant Hysteria': A letter reprinted from *The Times* of Thursday, 28 March 1912.
2. Hansard: HC Deb 20 May 1867, Vol 187 cc779-852. House of Commons, 20th May 1867, speech by John Stuart Mill.
3. *Paisley Herald and Renfrewshire Advertiser*, 26 April 1873.
4. ibid.
5. *Dundee Courier*, 7 November 1882.
6. *Aberdeen Press and Journal*, 23 December 1882.
7. *Dover Express*, 30 November 1866.
8. *Common Cause*, 21 November 1913.
9. Minute book of the Glasgow and West of Scotland Association for Women's Suffrage, May 1902.

10. *Women's Franchise*, 7 November 1907.
11. *The Suffragette*, 7 March 1913.
12. *Daily Record*, 5 May 1914.
13. *The Suffragette*, 19 December 1913.
14. *Votes for Women*, 5 December 1913.
15. *Votes for Women*, Friday, 5 November 1915.
16. *Votes for Women*, 23 January 1914.
17. ibid.
18. *Dundee Courier*, 11 October 1909.
19. *Dundee Courier*, 18 March 1914.
20. Minute book of the Glasgow and West of Scotland Association for Women's Suffrage.
21. *Jus Suffragii*, 1 November 1913.
22. 'The Citizenship of Women: A Plea for Women's Suffrage' a speech by J. Keir Hardie MP, published by Labour Party.

Chapter Five: Suffragettes: 'Fighting for my liberty'

1. John Cannon, *Oxford Dictionary of British History*. Published by Oxford University Press, 2015.
2. *Linlithgow Gazette*, 27 August 1909.
3. *An Appeal to Men*, by Victor D. Duval, October 1911.
4. *Dundee Courier*, 7 July 1914.
5. E. Sylvia Pankhurst, *The Suffragette Movement: An Intimate Account of Persons and Ideals*. Published 1931.
6. *Votes for Women*, 16 February 1912.
7. ibid.
8. *Daily Record and Mail*, 9 July 1914.
9. ibid.
10. ibid.
11. *The Suffragette Movement: An Intimate Account of Persons and Ideals*, by E. Sylvia Pankhurst, published 1931.
12. *The Courier*, 14 February 1907.
13. Elspeth King, *The Hidden History of Glasgow's Women*. Mainstream Publishing, 1993.
14. *The Suffragette*, 29 May 1914.
15. *The Suffragette*, 19 May 1914.

16. *The Suffragette*, 27 February 1914.
17. *The Scotsman*, 10 June 1913.
18. The *Aberdeen Daily Journal*, 8 March 1913.
19. *The Suffragette*, 13 December 1912.
20. The *Evening Telegraph and Post*, 18 December 1912.
21. *Daily Record and Mail*, 26 January 1914.
22. *Daily Record and Mail*, 26 January 1914.
23. *Aberdeen Press and Journal*, 10 August 1912.
24. The *Milngavie and Bearsden Herald*, 29 May 1914.
25. *Dundee Courier*, 25 May 1914.
26. *Daily Record and Mail*, 10 March 1914.
27. ibid.
28. *The Suffragette*, 20 March 1914.
29. ibid.
30. ibid.
31. *Glasgow Herald*, 12 March 1914.
32. *Daily Record and Mail*, 13 March 1914.
33. *Daily Record and Mail*, 20 November 1913.

Chapter Seven: War and work: 'An army of women'

1. *Jus Suffragii*, 1 February 1915.
 2. The *Common Cause*, 19 November 1915.
 3. ibid.
 4. *Jus Suffragii*, 1 September 1915.
 5. ibid.
 6. 'Women and the vote': parliament.uk/about/living- heritage/
    transformingsociety/electionsvoting/womenvote/overview/
    suffragetteswartime/
 7. *Yorkshire Evening Post*, 19 March 1915.
 8. *Yorkshire Evening Post*, 30 November 1915.
 9. 'Glasgow City Council: 100 years First World War
    Commemoration': firstworldwarglasgow.co.uk/index.
    aspx?articleid=10895
10. E. Morrison, C. Parry, 'The Scottish Women's Hospitals for
    Foreign Service – the Girton and Newnham Unit, 1915-1918':
    rcpe.ac.uk/sites/default/files/morrison_0.pdf

11. *Jus Suffragii*, 1 July 1915.
12. *Jus Suffragii*, 1 March 1915.
13. *Jus Suffragii*, 1 April 1915.
14. *British Medical Journal*, 17 February 1968.
15. *Daily Record and Mail*, 23 December 1915.
16. 'Glasgow City Council: 100 years First World War Commemoration': firstworldwarglasgow.co.uk/index.aspx?articleid=10895
17. *Jus Suffragii*, 1 November 1915.
18. *Daily Record and Mail*, 6 September 1915.
19. ibid.
20. 'Glasgow City Council: 100 years First World War Commemoration': www.firstworldwarglasgow.co.uk/index.aspx?articleid=11524
21. The *Glasgow Herald*, 19 September 1917.
22. Hansard: HC Deb 20 November 1917 Vol 99 cc1017-81017
23. 'Glasgow City Council: 100 years First World War Commemoration': www.firstworldwarglasgow.co.uk/index.aspx?articleid=11643
24. *Jus Suffragii*, 1 September 1915.
25. The *Glasgow Herald*, 19 March 1915.
26. *Votes for Women*, 6 October 1916.
27. The *Guardian*, 11 November 2008: www.theguardian.com/world/2008/nov/11/first-world-war-women-home-front
28. *Paisley and Renfrewshire Gazette*, 1 May 1897.
29. ibid.
30. *Dundee Courier*, 30 June 1934.
31. The *Scotsman*, 19 April 1934.
32. The *Glasgow Herald*, 2 June 1958.
33. *Daily Record and Mail*, 13 February 1939.
34. ibid.

Chapter Eight: Radical Women And The First Politicians: 'Fulfilling Hopes'

1. Fifteenth annual report Glasgow Society for Women's Suffrage 1916-17.

2. Hansard: HL Deb 10 January 1918 Vol 27 cc465-5.
3. Glasgow Society for Women's Suffrage Sixteenth Annual Report 1917-18.
4. Twentieth Annual Report, N.U.S.E.C Glasgow Society for Equal Citizenship 1921-22.
5. *Daily Record and Mail*, 8 October 1915.
6. ibid.
7. *Dundee Evening Telegraph*, 29 October 1915.
8. 'Remember Mary Barbour': remembermarybarbour. wordpress.com
9. *Daily Record and Mail*, 18 November 1915.
10. *Glasgow Herald*, 18 November 1915.
11. *Dundee Evening Telegraph*, 22 March 1911.
12. *The Vote*, 22 November 1918.
13. *Falkirk Herald*, 5 October 1918.
14. ibid.
15. Hansard: HC Deb 12 November 1937 Vol 328 cc2021-104.
16. 'Women and the Vote': parliament.uk/about/living-heritage/ transformingsociety/electionsvoting/womenvote/unesco/ equal-franchise-act-1928/
17. House of Commons Library: Women in Parliament and Government https://researchbriefings.parliament.uk/ ResearchBriefing/Summary/SN01250
18. Engender report: Sex & Power in Scotland 2017: https://www. engender.org.uk/content/publications/SEX-AND-POWER-IN-SCOTLAND-2017.pdf

Index